FOAL

Advance Praise for
Indulge Your Senses

"Simply put, Michael Dorf is a true hustler. When the internet upended the music business, he wasn't romantic to the way things were done and like any great entrepreneur, focused on what's happening today. It has been fun for me to watch Michael operate in this ever-changing world. There is a lot that can be learned from this man."

—GARY VAYNERCHUK, Founder and CEO, VaynerMedia;
and author, *Crushing It!*

"Music, wine, food, and community—not only has Michael Dorf cracked the code on a recipe so many of us crave most in an increasingly disconnected world, he's also managed to grow a brilliantly successful business while listening to his gut and sticking to his values. It's a feat that all entrepreneurs would be wise to study closely."

—DANNY MEYER, CEO, Union Square Hospitality Group;
Founder, Shake Shack; and author, *Setting the Table:
The Transforming Power of Hospitality in Business*

"The lessons learned in Michael Dorf's fascinating career make this as much a business book about how to thrive by indulging a customer's senses in our digital age as it is a gripping tale from an insider in the New York rock and jazz world during a period of massive technological change."

—STEVE CASE, co-founder of the investment firm
Revolution LLC and former CEO of AOL

"Sonic Youth, Beck, John Zorn, Cecil Taylor—Michael Dorf showcased them all at his cutting-edge Knitting Factory. Neil Young, Aaron Neville, Macy Gray, Shawn Colvin—those artists and more have graced his upscale City Winery. It's hard to imagine anyone in New York who has presented more great live music over the past thirty years. This book is the colorful story of how Dorf pulled it off, both before and after the Internet upended the music industry and changed our lives forever. It's inspiring reading for anybody who cares about music, culture, and wine, and explains how to thrive by offering people a live experience they will always remember."

—RITA HOUSTON, WFUV Program Director

INDULGE YOUR SENSES

SCALING INTIMACY
IN A DIGITAL WORLD

MICHAEL DORF

with Paul Keegan

Post Hill
PRESS

A POST HILL PRESS BOOK

Indulge Your Senses:
Scaling Intimacy in a Digital World
© 2019 by Michael Dorf
All Rights Reserved

ISBN: 978-1-64293-267-6
ISBN (eBook): 978-1-64293-268-3

Cover art by Cody Corcoran
Interior design and composition, Greg Johnson, Textbook Perfect

Post Hill Press
New York • Nashville
posthillpress.com

Published in the United States of America

"All our knowledge begins with the senses."

–IMMANUEL KANT

Contents

Acknowledgments

I was backstage at Carnegie Hall speaking with Patti Smith a few years ago, before one of my tribute concerts, and I asked her how she had such vivid recall in her incredible memoir, *Just Kids*, which I had just finished reading. She told me she had kept a diary, and, at that moment, I realized I was a big schmuck. I've had a pretty interesting life so far. I'm in my mid-fifties—and still have a lot more to do—but it occurred to me that, if I don't write a few things down, my memory will fade, and all those great stories will be lost forever.

So I started this project with my literary collaborator Paul Keegan, who had interviewed me for *Inc.* magazine. But this book is not a personal memoir like Patti's—I'm still way too young for that! Instead, I'm offering a timeline of my business journey so far: the many mistakes, trials, and tribulations, and lucky opportunities I've had, in hopes of providing a few good lessons for my fellow entrepreneurs—not to mention business executives, students, music fans, wine lovers, foodies, and really anyone interested in that place where business, technology, and culture meet. *Indulge*

Your Senses is my story of watching and participating in the incredible transformation of our world over the last forty years: the effects of digital technology not only on music, but on so much of society, and our very human need to connect with others around shared passions.

Absolutely none of this would have been possible without the incredible support of my family, including my grandparents and parents, who have been there every step of the way; my wife, Sarah, who, since college thirty-seven years ago (which is way more than half my life), has encouraged me, put up with my myopic and selfish drive to work, and filled in the gaps when I've been missing as a dad. My three kids are amazing and they, too, have all been understanding about my work/play, my hours, and my attempt to balance it all in this thing called "life." It's more than love; it's perhaps some unconscious shared gratitude and understanding that it could be so much worse—we could have been born centuries earlier and I'd be selling milk off a cart in Poland instead of wine and music in New York City. Anyway, deep, deep thanks to my family.

There are tons of other people who deserve thank-yous, and some names not put in the book, either because I forgot, there wasn't enough space, I was already name-dropping too much, or I was afraid of getting sued. But I wanted to single out my brother, Josh, who has been an incredible sounding board and unpaid adviser since he was in high school; my great team at City Winery doing the heavy lifting every day; my close friends from college; my mountain climbing pals; my golf friends; and the people I met in kismet airplane encounters over the years who have helped me think through this crazy puzzle of life.

I'd also like to thank my publicist, Michelle Fox, who was a catalyst in supporting the idea, hooking me up with the amazing Mollie Glick of Creative Artists Agency, who believed in this book when many others didn't; my publisher, Anthony Ziccardi of Post Hill Press, for taking a chance on my rather counterintuitive take on our digital age; Jacob Hoye for his fine and sensitive edit; copy editor Seane Thomas and proofreader Jon Blackwell for catching innumerable goofs, factual and otherwise; and my collaborator, Paul Keegan, for helping me turn my rambling stories into something coherent and, I hope, compelling.

Thank you all. If you bought this book, thanks so much. If I gave it to you for free, please tell me you loved it and are telling at least ten friends to go buy it. I need to cover the costs of my lawyers when somebody doesn't appreciate one of my jokes and drags my *tuchus* to court. *L'chaim.*

Introduction

How I Learned to Stop Worrying and Love Reality

I'll never forget the moment I began to feel that something big was happening—not just to me, but to the business world and American culture at large. And it all started with a hug from Joan Osborne.

It was New Year's Eve 2008, just a few months after the collapse of Lehman Brothers triggered the financial Armageddon that nearly wiped me out, along with just about everybody else on the planet. The timing was awful. I was trying to execute my crazy idea of building a live-music club in New York City with its own custom winery. That's right, we'd haul grapes in a refrigerated truck from world-class vineyards on the West Coast to Manhattan and make exquisite vintages right here on the premises.

We called it City Winery. It would have an intimate, 300-seat restaurant where customers could drink our fine wines and order a delicious meal, while enjoying concerts by artists such as Elvis Costello, Steve Earle, Suzanne Vega, and Esperanza Spalding. When the Great Recession hit, the winery had been completed in our building on the west side of SoHo in Manhattan (a stone's throw from Wall Street), the grapes had arrived, and construction crews were kicking up sawdust building the restaurant and performance stage. The failure rate of restaurants and music clubs is sky-high, even in the best of times, of course, and now we were suffering through a global economic meltdown. My forty-three limited partners who had entrusted me with $5 million were in no mood for excuses. Basically, I was screwed.

And yet the show had to go on. We had already booked Joan Osborne for opening night. Joan is amazing. Though most people know her from her huge hit "(What if God Was) One of Us," she is about so much more than that one great song. She's a powerful, bluesy singer, songwriter, and musical interpreter with a passionate following. Joan was exactly the type of artist we knew would appeal to our target demographic of affluent baby boomers.

Waiting for Joan to arrive, I was a bundle of nerves. But, hey, I'm used to it. At fifty-seven, I've been riding the emotional roller coaster of the music business for a long time. Growing up in Milwaukee, I had always loved music, but truly sucked as a musician myself. So at age twenty-three, I became manager of Swamp Thing, a band my friends had started. A couple of years later, I used my bar mitzvah savings to open a music cafe in New York called the Knitting Factory and convinced two high-school friends, Bob Appel and Louis Spitzer, to join me. Shockingly, our dumpy little club took off by presenting cutting-edge music by the likes of Sonic Youth, Beck, Cecil Taylor, Oliver Lake, and, later, Lou Reed. With its bare-bones aesthetic, The Knit became one of the hottest music scenes on the East Coast in the late '80s and '90s, allowing me to expand the record label I'd started and create branded music festivals in Europe.

Then the dot-com boom hit, and the music industry was turned upside down. After surviving the transition from vinyl to CDs, I was jazzed that music was now being liberated from its physical mooring altogether. I thought, "Why not plug into the internet so our shows can be heard by millions of people around the world?" In four investment rounds, we raised $5 million from some New York venture capitalists, partnered with Apple, Intel, Texaco, and Bell Atlantic, and I became one of those digital evangelists raving about how technology was going to change the world. We all know what happened next: The tech bubble burst, 9/11 hit, and the country plunged into a recession. In the scuffle, I lost control of the company to some slick Vulture Capitalists and ended up on my *tuchus* (that's "ass" in New York Yiddish).

Sure, I was down, but not out. By the time New Year's Eve 2008 rolled around, I was determined to make my comeback with City Winery—economic meltdown or no.

Fortunately, we had a sell-out crowd on opening night. (If I've learned anything over the years, it's how to fill a club with passionate music fans.) As the crew set up the stage, a lovely woman with curly blonde hair appeared and began fiddling around with the equipment. I realized that was Joan Osborne, preparing for her sound check.

Watching Joan work, I found myself remembering the mistakes I'd made in dealing with musicians over the years and thinking about how badly I wanted to do things right this time. At the Knitting Factory, I had become so preoccupied with selling our concerts around the world that I ignored the needs of artists who were actually making the music. In fact, I wasn't even calling it *music* anymore. Now it was *content*. A low point came when one of my idols, John Lurie of the Lounge Lizards, wrote an angry letter to *New Times Los Angeles* claiming that "Dorf is Frod backwards." I used to be so close to the musicians I loved. Now some of them wouldn't even look me in the eye.

So, when I started City Winery, I decided the club would not own any intellectual property. There would be no webcasting, no streaming, no recording of shows, period. I was tired of musicians looking at me like, *You got any more of my money in your pocket?* This time, we would invite customers into our room and simply let them experience the joy of live music by great artists. For the talent, the deal would be generous and straightforward: Most of the ticket revenue would go directly to the musicians, plus we would feed them a great meal with excellent and abundant wine. The vibes in our elegant, comfortable room with its state-of-the-art sound system would be awesome, for audiences and artists alike.

When she finished her sound check, Joan spotted me. Her face lit up, and suddenly, I had a good feeling about tonight. Hopping off the stage, she flung her arms wide and wrapped me in a bear hug. She thanked me for creating this wonderful space, one of the only rooms in New York—not to mention the rest of the country—where she could present her music in a warm, sophisticated setting. She didn't have to state the obvious: The gig was also worth her time and effort. First, internet piracy, then legal digital downloads, and now streaming services like Spotify had so thoroughly shattered the old music-business model that artists like her increasingly had to rely on live shows like this one to support themselves.

When the concert began, Joan did her thing. She was radiant in her long dress, casting her spell, pulling the audience in. Watching, I felt a lump in my throat and realized why her hug meant so much to me. My biggest sin over the years was not ambition, but letting technology interfere with the simple human exchange between artist and audience. That powerful, intimate joining of hearts is what I had always loved about music, and I'd lost it somewhere along the way—along with the bear hugs I used to get.

That night, the magic was back. Everyone in the room seemed to be sharing the same happy feelings I was experiencing. In the months and years that followed, we remained packed for every show, and, gradually, I began to understand why the high spirits of that evening continued, night after night: Joan's embrace was not just about my own absolution. Our whole culture was going through a similar reckoning.

By then, the smartphone and social-media revolution was underway, and I realized why music fans were showing up in droves. Like me, they had inadvertently let technology disrupt their connection to music—and now they were coming to City Winery to get *away* from their devices. They were eager to escape their hermetic digital bubble, excited to watch their favorite musicians pluck real guitar strings and slam actual drum skins while also nourishing their other senses—the dramatic sight of a legendary performer up close, the aroma of the winery, the taste of great food and wine, the touch of a nearby friend. We were offering the whole package in a supremely comfortable setting, a rarity in the live-music business, which leans toward impersonal stadiums and cramped dives with sticky floors.

We attracted people like Deborah Friedman, a political media consultant and contemporary art dealer, who has gone to about a hundred shows a year since we opened, seeing everyone from Graham Parker to Natalie Cole. Now retired, she has become close friends with dozens of other music fans she met at the club—they all tend to sit at the same tables together and stay in touch outside the club. "I feel like I'm part of the City Winery family, and, in forty-four years in Manhattan, I've never felt that way about any club or restaurant before," she says. "The community I've formed here is real. It's not a virtual community. I think, in a digitized world, that's something we all yearn for."

Eventually, I would create a PowerPoint presentation for our employees to illustrate that sense of community. It juxtaposed two images—one of a Bruce Springsteen concert, with rapturous fans waving their hands in the air; the other of a gospel church congregation doing exactly the same thing. Forgive me if this seems blasphemous, but I firmly believe both gatherings offer something that no technology can replicate: a kind of spiritual experience in a sacred place.

A great example of this occurred in August of 2013, when Prince was in town. We had already booked four sold-out nights with his band, The New Power Generation—but, as usual, there were no guarantees that Prince himself would show up. During the Friday night show, he actually circled the block in his car but, for whatever reason, decided not to come in. Then, on Sunday night, his band played a long, killer show and the concert appeared to be over. But, just after 3 a.m., the crowd let out a roar when His Badness himself strode onto the stage, dressed in black, wearing shades and a long gold-chain necklace. Prince proceeded to play a wild, thirty-two-song show with two encores. By the time he finished, it was nearly 6 a.m. Our delirious audience staggered out into the downtown dawn, sleep-deprived but totally energized, still high from his incredible performance (and the superb food and wine—I'm just sayin'). There's no app for that.

Within a few months of our opening, I realized that my initial hunch was correct: Having a fully functioning winery on the premises *did* differentiate us from other music clubs and restaurants and gradually helped us turn a profit. Our 300-person capacity seemed to hit a sweet spot rare in the live-music world—big enough to book famous artists but small enough to feel intimate. No sooner had we survived the financial crisis, however, than I was faced with another dilemma, this one about identity and branding. I couldn't shake the question, *What is City Winery, exactly?* A concert venue? A winery? A restaurant? A private event space? Since nothing like it existed anywhere in the world, there was no road map to follow.

I wrestled with this puzzle for quite a while—a truly existential conundrum—until I finally realized the answer was quite simple: "All of the above." But it wasn't until 2014 that I came up with three words that distilled our purpose into a single phrase:

Indulge Your Senses.

Creating that mantra was a big turning point because it gave our company a clear focus: We provide an oasis of sensory experience in an intimate setting, something you just don't find in other music spaces (or traditional restaurants and wineries, for that matter). But, in a world where apps can quickly deliver all the food, spirits, and electronic entertainment you could possibly desire directly to your home, was this just a quirky New York thing? How big was this market we had discovered? Was it actually possible to—if you'll forgive the apparent oxymoron—scale intimacy?

Our answer came soon enough. Four years after opening in New York, we cut the ribbon in Chicago and, today, we have locations in Nashville, Atlanta, Boston, and Washington, D.C. In the fall of 2019, we will be opening our seventh venue, in Philadelphia, as well as a gorgeous new winery/event space in a historic mill in upstate Montgomery, N.Y. (a brief foray into Napa Valley, the heart of California's wine country, was our only miss).

Most exciting of all, by early 2020, we will have moved our flagship Manhattan location to Pier 57, a new $400 million-plus mixed-use development on the Hudson River. With a large, stunning outdoor rooftop park and prestigious tenants like Google, this former maritime port will be home to our most ambitious City Winery yet. Over the next few years, we will continue to expand across the US and internationally, as we explore large urban areas like Los Angeles and London and smaller cities such as Toronto, Denver, and Detroit.

When City Winery began eleven years ago, I never imaged that the key to our success would be offering a proudly analog experience in an increasingly digital world. But that formula continues to work beautifully as we grow exponentially, and more investors come on board. Though it took us nine years to get to $50 million in revenue, it took us only two years to reach a projected $90 million in 2019, and we expect to hit $250 million by 2022. With double-digit operating profitability (earnings before interest, taxes, depreciation and amortization, or EBITDA), our seventy-five investors are happy to be receiving a very healthy return, which we re-invest in the company's growth. At this pace, we could easily reach thirty to forty locations in the United States, and as many as a hundred venues around the globe.

My hope, in writing this book, is to serve as an inspiration to fellow entrepreneurs, business leaders, students, and professionals who may not realize that, even in the digital age, you can create a thriving business or career by appealing to the human need to put our devices down, indulge our senses, and engage with one another on this beautiful planet.

Man, it feels great to be back in the real world.

🍇 🍇 🍇

Before I go any further, I'd like to be clear about what this book is *not* about. This is not a Luddite steampunk manifesto, or a screed against the modern world. I was one of the earliest pioneers of digital music in the late '80s and

'90s and still believe in the miraculous power of technology. Obviously, the internet has re-ordered the global economy, minted new billionaire demigods, and disrupted nearly every facet of modern life—none more powerfully than the world of music. There's no going back, nor would I ever want to.

Here's what I *am* saying: In our rush to adapt to the demands of the new world, business leaders have over-compensated to the point that anything carrying a whiff of analog is cast aside as hopelessly out of date, irrelevant to our future, and probably uncool to boot. As a wealthy venture capitalist once told me, "It's gotta be all digital or it's not worth doing." That is a big mistake. My counterargument is simple: As technology becomes more deeply woven into our lives, the key to success for many companies can be found in satisfying their customers' yearning for live human interaction.

We human beings are, after all, analog creatures. We are made of bone, blood, and sensitive nerve endings, so we naturally crave contact with the physical world. That translates into enormous business opportunities for anyone who understands that modern life has become a complex interplay between the world of atoms and the world of bits—and both are crucial to success. It's not an either/or proposition.

My own business provides a perfect example. Like everybody else, I rely on the internet to run my company and sell my services and products. But one of my biggest challenges is figuring out how to strike a harmonious balance between the two worlds we all inhabit—the real and the virtual.

I'm not saying it's easy. At City Winery, I made the difficult decision to forgo millions in revenue by not recording and streaming the performances on our stages because that would disrupt the delicate alchemy we have created—and could be seen as exploitive. On the other hand, we do allow fans to record our shows with portable devices, as long as it's not disruptive and the artist doesn't mind (most of them don't). That's a fine line to walk, but so far, that's the balance that feels right for us.

By now, the dangers of rushing to embrace an all-digital strategy are starting to become apparent. Even the greatest online retailer of them all, Jeff Bezos, realized that he could not succeed without physical stores—that's why Amazon bought Whole Foods Market, has opened bookstores, Amazon Go grocery stores, four-star stores (selling products that get at least a four-star Amazon rating) and is looking into selling furniture, home appliances, and other products offline. Take a look around and see how banks are becoming trendy cafes and entertainment giants are running thrill-packed theme parks, all to better connect with customers. Even as e-books, music streaming, and iPhone cameras have upended their industries, independent bookstores are doing well selling print books while vinyl records and film cameras are making a solid comeback. The $44 billion direct-mail industry continues to thrive, despite its high cost compared to email marketing, because those envelopes, cardstock flyers, and catalogs get people's attention. Meanwhile, artists of all stripes whose work has been digitized—from writers to visual artists to musicians—understand they need live events to reach their audiences.

If you think my argument is a generational thing, you may be right—but not in the way you might think. Younger generations actually seem to understand better than anyone how cool the Real World can be. As David Sax notes in his book, *The Revenge of Analog: Real Things and Why They Matter*, millennials are driving much of today's demand for non-digital products, from Moleskine notebooks to board games, and are demanding workplaces that encourage physical interaction. Nearly half of millennials worry about the negative effects of social media on their mental and physical health, according to the American Psychiatric Association. Middle-age consumers like me, meanwhile, love the idea of regaining something precious that's been lost in our mad dash toward a digital utopia. It appears the human longing for the physical is universal, regardless of age.

"Surrounded by digital, we now crave experiences that are more tactile and human-centric," Sax writes. "We want to interact with goods and services with all our senses, and many of us are willing to pay a premium to do so, even if it is more cumbersome and costly than its digital equivalent."

This last point is important because it gets at something I have noticed in my travels. As the market value of something decreases—recorded music, for example—people are willing to spend more for a similar product they consider superior. That's a big reason City Winery has been doing so well. People will pay fifty dollars for a ticket and at least that much for dinner and wine, because it's a far more luxurious experience than listening to music through earbuds or speakers. And that's as true for our affluent regular customers as those in lower income brackets who are splurging on a special night out. Analog is certainly more trouble—dressing up and traveling to one of our venues takes far more effort than chilling on the couch. But people will make that effort to get a sensory experience they may remember for the rest of their lives. That's why Broadway shows keep having one record-breaking year after another. (By comparison, our prices are a bargain.)

In the digital age, of course, companies must provide customers with a compelling reason to show up in person. If they do, the crowds will come. Companies that don't are suffering greatly. While Amazon has devoured the retail industry, chains like Macy's, Sears, and J.C. Penney are closing stores and laying off thousands of employees because they have failed to create an in-store experience inspiring enough to make people leave the comfort of their homes. In the music business, the now-defunct Tower and Virgin megastores had the same problem, never realizing that they had to evolve into music clubs/hangouts–anything, really, besides a seller of obsolete plastic discs.

At this point, you might be saying, "Yes, but aren't large segments of the economy still going purely digital, with no analog components at all?" The answer is yes, but even those companies understand the limits of ones and zeros. Two of China's largest companies–the video-game maker Tencent and the online shopping giant Alibaba–are, like Amazon, branching out into the sensory world with multibillion-dollar investments in brick-and-mortar supermarkets. People still want to squeeze the oranges.

And the "digital economy," though growing rapidly, is still not as big as one might think, comprising 30 percent of GDP in the US and just 5 percent worldwide. Despite Amazon's massive disruption of the economy, it's remarkable that online shopping still only accounts for about 10 percent of all retail sales in the US. Combine that with society's increasing skepticism about technology—fears about everything from device addiction and privacy violations to fake news and tech monopolies—and there are clearly tremendous opportunities for clever entrepreneurs and companies eager to satisfy our very human demand for the real thing.

As City Winery was taking off, I did some research to better understand the larger cultural shifts contributing to our success. Sales of recorded music have plunged since 1999, when Napster began allowing people to download MP3 files for free, and the legal digitization of music that followed significantly lowered the cost of listening for consumers. With the advent of YouTube and streaming services like Spotify, people are listening to more recorded music than ever but paying much less for it. Meanwhile, sales of concert tickets and wine have shot up dramatically over that same time period.

Seeing those charts was a crystalizing moment for me. No wonder City Winery shows were almost always sold out: The more awash in technology and digital distraction the world became, the more people wanted to take time to unplug their earbuds, silence their ringers, and indulge themselves with live music and great food and wine alongside other fans. Spending less on recorded music freed up cash for consumers to spend on the kind of sensory experiences we offered. For our younger customers, the chance to show off to their friends using social media provides an added incentive to get out of the house.

As surprising and counterintuitive as this dynamic may sound, it's hardly a new development. Technology has been giving people an alternative to live music since the invention of the phonograph in the late 19th century. Back then, people could say, "Why go out when you can just slap a record on the Victrola?" But no machine has yet managed to dampen the human desire to hear those beautiful sounds coming directly from the artists who create them. And, until some genius discovers how to digitize wine and food—not to mention the romance and fun that comes with a night on the town—well, I think we'll have a great market for that as well.

As you'll see, this book is organized with chapter headings that lay out the hard-earned lessons I've learned as an entrepreneur during a lifetime of dramatic technological change, each one illustrated by examples from other companies and trend-setters, from Apple to Ziggy Stardust. I hope you'll dig hearing about my wild ride through the dot-com boom, suffering through the bust, and coming back with City Winery, all spiced with colorful anecdotes about famous folks I have encountered along the way, people like Lou Reed, Quincy Jones, John Zorn, and even Leonardo DiCaprio (who was my best friend for a few hours).

What a long, strange trip it's been. Enjoy.

1

Come Together

Creating a community of passionate customers—or *fans*, as we call them in the music industry—is the Holy Grail for any business, and today that process is faster and cheaper than ever before. But it's also become far too easy to see customers as disembodied bits or aggregated data points rather than actual people with needs and feelings.

Steve Jobs understood this problem well. That's why he created Apple Stores, a place to congregate, hold and feel the latest devices, and get problems solved by real human beings. Within three years of its launch in 2001, Apple Stores reached $1 billion in sales, the fastest growth in retail history. For all the miracles of distant connections, Jobs knew something that I have also realized: It's just as important to gather people together in live settings where they can satisfy their desires (indulge their senses), gather in modern places with

old-fashioned touches like wood tables and floors, and interact in spontaneous and joyful ways.
   In other words, throw a party.

It's almost comical that we have to relearn such basic truths of human motivation and behavior. When I was growing up in Wisconsin in the 1960s and '70s, the words "social" and "media" had never met. Gathering in person was all we knew, especially when it came to sharing music. From the Pete Seeger and Bob Dylan tunes we sang around the campfire at our socialist summer camp to the Jewish hymns at synagogue to the rock songs blasting from my friends' electric guitars, music always seemed like the most powerful force on the planet for bringing people together.

Like many kids, I took music lessons—two years of guitar—but I really sucked. Then again, I didn't come from a family of musicians. We were entrepreneurs, through and through, starting with Grandpa Sol who started the Milwaukee Biscuit Company in the 1940s. He was my dad's father and quite an operator in nearby Chicago, where he was raised; some old photos make it appear that Sol was hanging out with Al Capone, and I wouldn't be surprised if he moved plenty of hooch during Prohibition. (He and my Grandma had a "happy hour" every day into their nineties for as long as I can remember.)

As the oldest, my dad was next in line to take over the family business, which grew into a specialty food company with more than 5,000 products and $50 million in revenue.

But my father had just enough differences with his brother, Uncle Stan, that they decided to sell the company rather than allow the next generation to be burdened by family strife. That generation included me, my younger sister and brother, and three cousins.

I'm still grateful for that wise decision. Instead of training to be a company executive, with my destiny handed to me on a silver platter, I learned to become a scrappy entrepreneur who cooked up his own schemes. Dad and Grandpa Sol always supported my ventures, from my snow-shoveling business to the beer-can collection I started at age twelve (and merged with a friend's collection and sold for a tidy profit a year later). An interest in architecture, design, and construction work led me to team up with my friend Louis Spitzer to build rec rooms for our neighbors when we were teenagers.

My greatest triumph, however, came at the Seven Mile Fair, a flea market south of Milwaukee, just over an hour from Chicago. At first, nobody was buying our cookies from the Milwaukee Biscuit Company that my friend Todd and I tried to sell at three packs for a dollar. After we accidentally crushed some by sitting on a box, we marked them down as damaged goods and were shocked that they sold out immediately at "Five for a buck!" Excited, we broke the rest of the cookies on purpose. They sold like crazy. After that, I brought all kinds of damaged products from my Dad's company to the fair—dented cans, frozen olive oil, more broken cookies, you name it. I made thousands of dollars per weekend that way, eventually hiring my brother, cousins, and friends to keep up with demand. It was a valuable lesson: *Make do with what you have and make people feel they're getting a very special deal.*

Back then, music as a business was not on my radar. I was just a teenager looking for a way to fit in—a short, pimply kid who yearned to be cool and attract girls. I desperately wanted to be in a band, but I couldn't even play the simple opening riff from "Smoke on the Water" by Deep Purple: Bahm-bahm-bahm, bahm-bahm-ba-screech! The next best thing was to hang out with my friends who were great musicians, like Bob Appel. Bob could hear an Elton John song for the first time and, the next minute, play and sing it perfectly. Harlan Steinberger was like that, too, a real natural. They took the spotlight while I, a bit envious, worked behind the scenes as the sound man and lighting guy. I even built a lighting console with my cousin Mitch for the junior prom. I was the guy kinda in the band, hoping to get laid.

While Harlan eventually moved to LA and became a successful studio owner/musician, Bob and I hooked up again a few years later when he asked me to manage Swamp Thing, a band he was in while attending the University of Wisconsin at Madison. By then, I had my degree in psychology and business from Washington University in St. Louis, was living in Spain on a postgraduate year abroad, studying art, and wondering what to do with my life. Missing the states and my friends, I told Bob, "Yes, absolutely." In college, I had read the book *Hit Men: Power Brokers and Fast Money Inside the Music Business* by Fredric Dannen and thought being a music mogul sounded exciting. Then I did what many young people with no plausible way to support themselves do: I convinced my parents to pay for law school.

I was sort of interested in intellectual property rights and all that, but the main reason I enrolled at UW-Madison was to get room and board paid for while I managed Swamp Thing. The band was popular in small bars in Madison but had much bigger ambitions. My job was to make them rock stars. Armed with a hundred copies of the band's demo cassette, I hopped in my car and drove to New York City, stopping along the way at clubs in places like Milwaukee, Chicago, and Ann Arbor, Michigan, to drop off tapes. Somehow, I managed to book fifteen shows over six weeks during that summer of 1985.

Swamp Thing was not an overnight sensation, or any other kind of sensation, for that matter. Our first show at CBGB, Manhattan's famously dumpy punk mecca, paid exactly $22.50. After paying for posters ($35), meals that night ($25), and gas to drive from Wisconsin ($125), we lost $162.50. It was my first exposure to the brutalities of the music business. An uptown club called Trax even made us put down a hundred-dollar deposit and predict the number of people who would show up. I told them a hundred, but only nine came (another fifteen got in free on the guest list), so the club kept most of the deposit. By the end of the tour, we were $1,500 in the hole. If Visa hadn't extended my credit line, we would have been stuck on the East Coast, living on the streets.

Such setbacks didn't keep us from launching the band's new label, Flaming Pie Records. Swamp Thing's lead singer, Jonathan Zarov, came up with the name. He was a funny guy, a cross between David Byrne and Elvis Costello, but nerdier than both. He didn't have a great voice but wrote some memorable songs. (Sample lyric: "You can take your taxes and stick 'em up your asses!") The band was a lot of fun, with Bob and Jonathan on guitars, Michael Kashou on bass, and Steve Bear on drums. Swamp Thing's demo tape was rejected by every record label we could find—major and independent, big and small—so we decided to press the disc ourselves. (Yes, kids, that was back in the days of vinyl LPs.) We made a thousand copies of *Learning to Disintegrate* and used various distribution companies to get the album into stores. After all that work, we sold a total of 783 copies worldwide, mostly at gigs.

Being a band manager, I was learning, was an expensive proposition. Though some gig revenue trickled in, more money went out, and I usually made up the difference from my savings plus family loans that were never paid back. One big cost was putting out a string of records under the Flaming Pie label, including *The Mad Scene*, a compilation of songs by Madison-area bands that featured everything from old-fashioned rock and roll and blues to new wave and alternative music by bands like Phil Gnarley and the Tough Guys. (Their tune "Beer on My Breath," went like this: "Fuck the homework, let's get drunk!")

It was a crazy, fertile scene, and I'm still amazed at how many of its people went on to do big things. The studio work for *The Mad Scene* was done by Butch Vig, who later produced Nirvana's masterpiece, *Nevermind.* And the guy I replaced as the manager of Swamp Thing, Richard Lovett, would become president of one of the biggest talent firms in the world, Creative Artists Agency. (I still kid Richard that he's pretty good at managing talent, but never accomplished half as much as I did as agent and manager for Swamp Thing.)

Even though I was taking a bath financially, by the end of my first year of law school, I was hooked. This was fun! As opposed to law school, which wasn't. So I dropped out. Finally, at age twenty-four, my direction was clear: I would become a record producer.

Though I didn't realize it at the time, I was learning important lessons about technology and human interaction. You can sell a facsimile of an experience—a record album, for example—but the reproduction can never replace the magic of the original experience itself. The records I was trying to get radio stations to play did not come close to capturing the sensation of seeing the band live, the fun, or Jonathan literally climbing the walls of a club to entertain the audience. That's something that the business world should keep in mind as more aspects of our lives are replaced by digital representations. In my industry, capturing songs in a recording is a wonderful way to spread them far and wide—and helps musical innovations flourish. But music also needs to breathe in the open air, allowing listeners to connect directly to the creators of those magnificent sounds. Without that, something essential is missing. That's true not only in music, but in so many areas of our lives, as we increasingly work, socialize, shop, and entertain ourselves online and through screens.

I wasn't able to articulate any of these ideas in the spring of 1986, of course. All I knew was that I had to get out of Wisconsin. I loved the big cities on the East Coast and decided to head for New York to make my mark as a music impresario. (It also would allow me to be closer to my college sweetheart; more about Sarah later.) I found a small apartment in the East Village on 10th Street that became a crash pad for Swamp Thing during its tours, not to mention a cluttered warehouse for their gear and a mounting inventory of Flaming Pie records.

Around this time, Swamp Thing recorded its second album, this time at a studio in Connecticut. Our endlessly inventive singer, Jonathan, wanted to call it *Mr. Bloodstein's Knitting Factory*, inspired by the name of a sweater factory in Wisconsin where Bob had worked a few years back. We ended up calling it A *Cow Comes True*, but a cash cow, it was not. Borrowing money again from my grandfather Sol— still supportive of my entrepreneurial endeavors—we spent about $15,000 to make a record that brought in a whopping $4,000 in sales.

Before long, I hit rock bottom. All told, I'd probably sunk $40,000 into Flaming Pie Records with almost nothing to show for it. My career made no sense: Why was I going broke in New York when I could easily make a thousand dollars in a single weekend at the Seven Mile Fair? I was about to call it quits and head back to Wisconsin with my tail between my legs when I came up with one last, desperate idea to keep my dream alive of making it in the music business.

It was an old idea, actually, one I had discussed with my friend Lou Spitzer many times over cappuccinos: open a performance space and art gallery in New York City. Combing through *The Village Voice* classifieds, I found an old Avon Products office at 47 E. Houston Street that seemed like a steal at $1,800 a month. The location was perfect, between

Mott and Mulberry Streets, not far from CBGB and The Bottom Line.

The space was a former heroin den that needed lots of work—plaster chipping off the walls, a rotted wood toilet, piles of Avon products scattered across the floor. Lou and I had such a great partnership building rec rooms back in high school—he was good at carpentry and ceiling work, while I handled electricity and plumbing—that I convinced him to move to New York, stay at my apartment, and go into business with me. This was exciting: If the profits could support Flaming Pie Records, I might become a music mogul after all.

Borrowing from family (again) and using savings from my bar mitzvah gifts and Seven Mile Fair ventures, the project cost $75,000 and took five months. When it was done, not everyone shared our excitement. Even after our renovations, the floors were unfinished, the lighting cheap and minimal, the heating and air conditioning unreliable, and—there's no polite way to say this—it was still kind of a shithole. After we signed the lease, my parents came to visit. My mom took one look around, said, "Oh, my God!" and started crying.

We didn't care much about the rawness of the place. To me, that only added to its unpretentious charm. And the other tenants in the four-story walk-up were colorful characters, making it feel like a quintessential New York scene. The ground floor was Estella's Peruvian Restaurant. We occupied 2,000 square feet on the first floor and a large Hispanic family lived directly upstairs. On the third floor was an eccentric photographer named Ray in a horribly messy apartment with about twenty cats.

Our plan was to make the joint an art gallery by day; at night, it would be a center for jazz, poetry, performance art, or whatever we felt like booking. It would have an artistic, beatnik vibe, and we'd sell tea, coffee, and cookies. At first, I wanted to call it Expressoism. Then I was convinced it should be The Fire Escape, Inc. Friends wisely talked me out of both ideas. Then I remembered the original name for Swamp Thing's last album, so I called Jonathan and said, "Hey, can we call our new club *Mr. Bloodstein's Knitting Factory*?" He agreed, as long as I promised to buy him dinner sometime. (Jonathan, I still owe you!)

Then I got the idea to change the name every month to, say, Yonah Schimmel's Knitting Factory, or Charlie Smith's Knitting Factory, just to be funny and different (in fact, our first checks were printed with "_____'s Knitting Factory"). That got awfully confusing, so we decided to just call it the Knitting Factory.

We opened our doors in February of 1987 and the first band to play there was—who else?—Swamp Thing, attended by about twenty friends from Madison.

Yes, it was an inauspicious beginning, but fate was smiling on us. In our naivete, we had no idea that the New York music scene was ripe for a new venue like ours. There were high-end clubs like The Blue Note and the Village Vanguard offering straight-ahead jazz by established names. But that left out a whole constellation of talented New York musicians: those influenced by world beat and funk, free-jazz players, and instrumentalists who didn't fit neatly into any tidy definition of what jazz should be. In the rock world, there was hardly any adventurous programming beyond CBGB, leaving so many of those on the fringes of the rock, funk, country, and folk worlds without a home.

A singer/songwriter named Paul McMahon helped lead some of the rock and folk musicians to us. These quirky, talented artists were all happy to have a place to play, and by the end of April, nearly every night was booked. In those pre-internet days, I promoted the club by getting the home addresses of our customers and sending them a calendar of events. Then I ran around putting posters up on telephone poles, construction sites, lampposts, mailboxes, anything that didn't move.

We still didn't have any jazz, so I answered a classified ad by a pianist named Wayne Horvitz, who politely informed me that I didn't know what the hell I was doing and offered to program a jazz series on Thursday nights. He promised to fill the club in exchange for a seventy-five-dollar guaranteed fee for the artists and our pledge to blanket the area with posters. Great plan, but not enough people came. So I hatched a scheme to draw a crowd by assembling an exhibit of jazz photographs by Raymond Ross, the peculiar sixty-eight-year-old man who lived upstairs with all those cats.

Seeing Ray on the street, you might have mistaken him for a bum who looked like Jerry Garcia. But strewn across the floor of his apartment were thousands of priceless negatives and 8 x 10 prints, all stunning shots of legendary jazz musicians from the late 1940s to the '60s. To hype the exhibit, and the club, I created posters with photos and bold headlines that said things like, "Coleman Hawkins and Thelonious Monk during April." If people showed up at the Knitting Factory expecting to hear these immortals play, I explained that, alas, they were long dead but why not stay to hear the Jemeel Moondoc Quartet? An ethical breach, perhaps, but we didn't get many complaints. People were either too embarrassed or thought the whole thing was funny.

On the first night of our Thursday jazz series, I met the pioneering composer and saxophonist John Zorn, who said he was looking for a place to premier a new project called *Hu Die* that also featured the guitarists Bill Frisell and Fred Frith and a narrator reading in Korean. Um...okay, sounds great! We arranged for a special midnight show that gave us our first line out the door. We only had forty chairs, but ninety-five paid to get in that night—and Zorn brought twenty-five guests, mostly Japanese women. Those 120 people, squished in like sardines, hot and sweaty, were the most beautiful thing I had ever seen.

We were off and running. Maybe it was Ray's jazz photographs, but a spiritual vibe seemed to be taking over the place. (A woman who called herself the High Priestess, who was dating the owner of the building, claimed that she had burned certain herbs in the building to summon us to rent it.) The press would later dub us "a mecca for downtown music" for featuring still-obscure groups like Sonic Youth, Indigo Girls, and They Might Be Giants, an early show by Beck, and avant-garde jazz musicians such as Anthony Braxton, Cecil Taylor, Don Cherry, Dewey Redman, and Oliver Lake. John Lurie of the Lounge Lizards, who had recently appeared in Jim Jarmusch's film *Down by Law*, told *New York* magazine that, because the city's club scene was so conventional, "If you were doing anything interesting at all, it guaranteed you failure. The Knitting Factory re-invoked the music scene in New York."

I wish I could say I had some grand vision about which acts to bring in. Truth is I didn't have a clue. I just booked whatever I liked, or whatever sounded interesting (most of what I knew about jazz came from a single college history-of-jazz class). I loved the concept of having a Jack Kerouac beatnik vibe, and the New York music scene was so diverse, vivacious, and exciting, it was hard to focus on any single genre. Our brochure said we offered "sort of improvised-new music-rock-jazz-classical-funk-hardcore-hip-hop stuff." That pretty much covered it.

The musicians, meanwhile, liked the fact that we gave them 75 percent of the ticket price. So, if a hundred people came and paid $10 each, the band got $750 straight up, no hidden fees. Word soon spread that some naive sucker on Houston Street was paying good money, so an incredible range of artists flocked to us. As Zorn later said in an interview, "We fed it and it fed us, and it became bigger than both of us."

Sometimes my musical instincts were way off. A handsome New Orleans singer and pianist who had rented an apartment across the street handed me a demo tape, but I told him he was too mainstream for The Knit. Then the soundtrack to *When Harry Met Sally* came out and Harry Connick, Jr. blew up. Eventually, he sold 28 million records worldwide, making me feel like a complete idiot—a principled idiot, perhaps, but an idiot nonetheless.

And when the lead singer of an obscure Vermont band gave me a demo tape, I said his group sounded too much like The Grateful Dead. "We don't do Dead music here," I sniffed. Trey Anastasio soon landed a gig at the Wetlands Preserve in Tribeca and *Rolling Stone* would later call Phish "the most important band of the '90s." Trey was gracious about the whole thing, telling me that he respected my integrity, but that's far too charitable an explanation for my stupidity. (Fortunately, it was a forgivable sin: I later became friends with Phish's bass player, Mike Gordon, who had a birthday party/jam session at City Winery soon after we opened in 2008.)

At the time, I didn't think of the Knit as being strictly a music club. That seemed too narrow to me. So I booked artists like the influential drag performer Ethyl Eichelberger and another great queen, Joey Arias, who would pack the joint doing the music of Billie Holiday. (We even made a disc with him on Flaming Pie Records.) I loved those artists for attracting an entirely different crowd than the rockers and avant-garde musicians. We also had lots of art hanging on the walls in those early years; some pieces came from bartered drinks or in lieu of my commission when we sold something. We also built a runway to present fashion shows, some of them pretty strange. That was fine with me. I was game for just about anything.

As crowds began to form in our little club, I knew it was not because of the food, which sucked—avocado-and-cream-cheese sandwiches, tabbouleh salad, hummus, etc. It was not about the beer (cheap) or wine (none). It was not about the space—a dump that was too hot in the summer, too cold in the winter, and had only one bathroom. At age twenty-four, I didn't care about such creature comforts anyway, and figured most of our audience didn't either. (All that would come later, with City Winery.)

The magic inside the walls of the Knitting Factory was happening because of the community we were creating. People came for the artistic, adventurous scene, a place where they could enjoy the warm vibe and connect with other lovers of music and art. It was a place where musicians felt welcome, where their fans enjoyed hanging out, and where nobody had to worry about dirtying an ashtray. The lesson I had learned at the Seven Mile Fair with those broken cookies was true: *Make do with what you have and make people feel they're getting a very special deal.* In this case, they were getting a very special experience.

Most importantly, this was a place I'd love to go myself. (If entrepreneurs don't love the product they are offering, their customers will feel it.) I hated dance clubs with thumping music and flashing lights, even if I could have made it past the velvet rope, which I couldn't. I was a short Jew with no money or connections, not a stud easing past bouncers to pick up chicks. I wanted the Knitting Factory to feel completely accessible and friendly, with no lines at all. So I treated our customers just the way I'd want to be treated, greeting them at the door, sitting them down, and asking what they wanted to eat or drink. Maybe it was just instinctive Midwestern Nice, but the fabled restaurateur Danny Meyer of Shake Shack fame (who had opened his Union Square Cafe two years earlier) has a great phrase for it: "Enlightened Hospitality," a motto we later adopted at City Winery. That approach turned out to be a big part of the Knitting Factory's appeal.

Making money, on the other hand, was a trickier proposition. I was so broke that I gave up my apartment on East 10th Street and slept on a futon under my desk in our office in the back of the club. I went to Pineapple Fitness around the corner every morning to shower, brush my teeth, and shave (never actually working out, though I did take an occasional steam). When the beer delivery came at 10 a.m., I was there to greet them in my underwear. Fortunately, I was young, with no obligations, and having a great time. Riches and a cushy lifestyle could wait.

Today, it's funny to look back and read the image that *New York* magazine writer Phoebe Hoban paints in her 1989 story about the founding of the Knitting Factory, appropriately entitled "Knit Wits": "Dorf scratches a day's growth of beard. He looks like a college kid who's stayed up all night finishing a term paper. He favors baggy shorts or drawstring pants, mismatched socks, and an odd assortment of T-shirts. It's not that he doesn't have ambition; but he couldn't care less about Attitude. He's no [trendy club owners] Steve Rubell or Rudolf or Eric Goode. He's more like Beaver Cleaver as an artsy entrepreneur."

As we struggled to pay the rent, we were learning why no club like the Knitting Factory existed in New York. As a for-profit business, we could not rely on the funding and grants that non-profits typically receive to present such risky avant-garde shows. And we often had more people on the guest list—musicians, artists, journalists, music industry types—than paying customers.

But our approach did create fantastic buzz. One night, I got to meet my hero David Byrne, who came to hear Cecil

Taylor. Debbie Harry and Peter Gabriel stopped by, and so did Willem Dafoe on the night his film *The Last Temptation of Christ* opened. As word spread, music fans loved knowing such famous artists might show up at any time.

Music critics were also ecstatic. In *The Nation*, Gene Santoro called us "an indispensable part of the music scene in New York City," and Britain's 20/20 *Time Out* magazine said we had "arguably the most vital collision of musical sounds heard in America. Or anywhere for that matter." Just three months after we opened, Peter Watrous of *The Village Voice* said, "they *are* the scene." We were pinching ourselves. Could they really be talking about *us*?

A few months after we opened, my old friend Bob Appel reappeared. Swamp Thing had still not broken through and he was trying to figure out what to do next. It was great timing. We desperately needed help, especially in areas Bob excelled in—working our sound system and handling musicians. By then, Louis had tired of the nightly grind. He was an artist and craftsman, not a slinger of drinks, and our art gallery never took off. (We only sold one painting, for $200, earning a whopping $80 in commissions.) In came Bob and out went Louis, along with my endless gratitude to Louis for getting the club up and running.

As a musician, Bob was used to hanging out at dumpy nightclubs. And he understood, far better than me, how important the artists were to our whole enterprise. So, between keeping musicians happy, running sound, and infusing the place with his smiles and positive attitude, Bob became a terrific partner and a big key to our success.

Though it took a while for our business model to pay off, it was ahead of its time in one respect. In those days, popular artists played live shows to promote their records, which generated most of their revenue. Our setup was just the opposite, with the Knitting Factory's live shows producing far more sales than Flaming Pie Records. In fact, The Knit was initially conceived to support the record label. That's more like the way things are today, when many artists earn more from live performances than recordings.

Back then, it was impossible for Flaming Pie Records to get the attention of big radio stations or the major labels. The barriers to entry were simply too high, so it made more sense to create a physical space for people to hear music—with paper dollars and credit cards at the ready to buy tickets and drinks—and make *that* the foundation of the business. First, create a passionate community of fans, and then try to sell them products—recordings, food, drinks, T-shirts, whatever. At the time, it seemed like a natural progression.

When I named the club the Knitting Factory, I loved that it was an oxymoron, melding together opposing concepts of the handmade and the automated. It was absurd. How could something knitted be produced by a factory? But, like a Zen koan, or a brilliantly improvised piece of music, the name provoked a response deeper than thought, creating a paradox that cannot be resolved solely through logic. And that's precisely where our relationship between the real and the digital exists today, in a world that is simultaneously physical and virtual, both yin and yang.

Figuring out how to bring these two apparent opposites together in harmony, in my view, is one of the central challenges for any business today. It's fascinating to watch companies exploring that frontier. Disney is a good example, having turned its film properties into live events at hugely profitable theme parks and with shows like Disney on Ice, *The Lion King*, and Marvel superhero arena events. The world of Harry Potter has become a big moneymaker, beyond the books and movies, as a physical experience at Universal Parks & Resorts. Bringing people together, the entertainment giants have discovered, makes more business sense today than ever before.

Back on East Houston Street, as we entered the final decade of the 20th Century, we had no clue about any of this. Bob and I were just kids in our mid-twenties. All we knew was that something big was happening in the music business called "digital," and we had to quickly learn how to integrate it into the mad, ecstatic, serious, hilarious, pioneering downtown music club I had, almost accidentally, created.

2

Embrace Ch-ch-ch-ch-changes

Embracing both the real and the virtual has never seemed like a contradiction to me. At City Winery, we've always used social media, email, texts, and our heavily trafficked website—far more than conventional advertising—to bring customers to our venues, where they can immerse themselves in the rich sensory world we have created.

This duality is common in the live-entertainment business, but other industries can benefit tremendously from an artful weaving of analog and digital, especially retailers trying to bring customers into their stores in the age of Amazon. A Neiman Marcus app, for example, allows users to take a picture of a pair of shoes in the store. The app produces a range of similar styles and matching handbags for purchase online or at the register. In the end, it's all about the best way to serve the customer.

The trick for all businesses is knowing when to adopt a new piece of technology and when to wait it out. This can be a tough call, and a big risk either way. Fortunately, the music industry offers revealing examples of the right and wrong ways to handle it.

David Bowie was one of the first artists to "turn and face the strange," as he urged in his hit "Changes." Though he chased some dead ends, like interactive CD-ROMs, Bowie had an uncanny track record of early adoption, becoming the first pop star to offer MP3 downloads and develop his own website (a primitive, text-based beast). It burnished his reputation as a fearless risk-taker and allowed him to reach more fans. Other artists such as David Byrne, Prince, Kristin Hersh, and Todd Rundgren blazed similar trails.

The wrong response to a gestating tech revolution is to stick your head in the sand—or, worse, hire a bunch of lawyers to fight it. That's what the Big Six record labels did, trying to stop the home recording of CDs and then putting their fingers in the dikes as digital downloads and streaming models gained momentum. Record retailers were also oblivious. "Is this really something consumers will want?" a Tower Records executive was quoted as saying about downloads in 1998. "I think going to the record store is a communal thing."

Oy vey! The results of wearing such blinders were devastating. Today, the record industry is about half the size it was at its peak in 1999. The Big Six is down to the Big Three, and retail chains like Tower went bankrupt—a poignant case study in how *not* to deal with an existential threat to your business model. (Hint: Change your business model.)

On these matters, I speak from experience. As the Knitting Factory took off in the late '80s and early '90s, I had to choose between joining the Brave New World of digital music or ignoring it and focusing on the live shows that paid the rent. Without hesitation, I jumped headlong into the world of ones and zeros. In retrospect, that turned out to be the right call. (My regrets—yes, I had a few—came later.) For me, it was mostly youthful enthusiasm for something new and exciting. When we bought our first live-streaming box, we started getting emails from Singapore saying things like, "I was just on my 14.4-baud modem, listening to live music from the Knitting Factory!" That did it. I was like, "Oh, my God, Watson!"

In some ways, technology is like fine wine. In the right amounts, under the right circumstances, both can enhance our lives immeasurably. As the Greek playwright Aristophanes said a couple thousand years ago, "'Tis when men drink they thrive—grow wealthy, speed their business, win their suits, make themselves happy, benefit their friends." Yes, absolutely. A cool piece of software can do that too.

Like wine, tech can also dramatically alter our perception of reality. One of my earliest inklings about the coming future shock arrived courtesy of Nicholas Negroponte, the academic who, in 1985, started the Media Lab at the Massachusetts Institute of Technology in Cambridge, just a four-hour drive up I-95 from New York. His book, *Being Digital*, was a revelation, explaining that a fundamental transformation was occurring as society shifted from the world of atoms to the world of bits—weightless, disembodied pieces of computer code that moved at the speed of light. When I met him years later, he illustrated this phenomenon by looking dismissively at the Knitting Factory business card I handed him. "Oh, I don't have cards anymore," he said. "I'm done with atoms." As he rattled off his email address, I fumbled to write it down—with pen and paper, of course.

In my industry, the shift from atoms to bits had already begun. The same year Negroponte started the Media Lab, Dire Straits became the first artist to sell a million albums on CD, marking the beginning of the end for analog media—i.e., those vinyl Flaming Pie records I was desperately trying to sell for my buddies in Swamp Thing.

Not that I really understood any of this when we opened the Knitting Factory in early 1987. I was still an analog kid: In the mornings, after waking up under my desk, I would resume my day job of promoting my Wisconsin bands, calling college radio stations and saying, "Hey, I've got this great new LP by Phil Gnarley and the Tough Guys!" I could practically hear them yawning on the other end until I mentioned that I also had a club in New York that booked artists like Bill Frisell and Sonic Youth. Suddenly, they perked up. "Got any recordings? Now *that* we would play!"

So I got to work creating a series of cassette tapes called *Live at the Knitting Factory* and, eventually, 250 college radio stations around the country signed up. The artists agreed to let us record them because we weren't selling the tapes. This was strictly a promotional tool to attract fans to the club. That helped the musicians sell more tickets and helped us sell more beer. The radio stations would mention our brand several times an hour between songs by, say, the singer Cassandra Wilson or jazz saxophonist Steve Coleman. The series became so popular that TDK agreed to sponsor us with a small fee and all the free cassette tapes we could handle. Once we got rolling, my partner Bob practically lived in the studio making hundreds of copies on six double-cassette decks that he wired together to duplicate faster.

Live at the Knitting Factory was not only an incredible marketing tool; it also provided us with a big incentive to go digital. Now that we were taping these phenomenal musicians—recordings we hoped might someday be as valuable as those old Blue Note or Verve jazz sessions—I wanted the best equipment possible. In those days, that meant a DAT machine. Sony had just come out with the Digital Audio Tape recorder a few months earlier, claiming it had a sampling rates up to 48 kHz, at 16 bits of quantization. Whatever. All I knew was that it was the latest thing, the wave of the future, and I wanted one—badly. The problem was that DAT machines cost thousands of dollars.

One day, I was walking on the Bowery—the sidewalk jammed with hustlers selling their wares—when I spotted a guy offering a big, heavy DAT recorder for just $200. It was obviously stolen, but I immediately started rationalizing: *Hey, if I don't buy it, he'll just sell it to some other schmuck. I didn't tell him to swipe it or fence it for whoever did.*

I bought it and excitedly carried my new toy back to the club. The device was as fantastic as advertised, easy to use, with awesome sound quality. Sadly, a few months later, while we were away on a camping trip, some burglars smashed a hole through our exterior wall and rammed through the concrete masonry. They crawled inside, opened the front door, and walked out with everything we had—house sound system, recording equipment, and, of course, my shiny new DAT recorder. The karmic irony of my hot machine getting stolen was hard to miss. Eventually, I realized what my first digital contact high had done: I was behaving like an addict, skewing my moral compass.

Now we were really fucked. Fortunately, we had built up so much good will among musicians in the months since we opened that we managed to organize a long day of benefit concerts at the elegant Puck Building a few doors down. John Lurie and the Lounge Lizards were the headliners, but many other legendary musicians showed up to play, including John Zorn, the saxophonist/flutist Oliver Lake, and the drummer Rashied Ali.

That event, in October of 1987, was a phenomenal success. Not only did we raise a large sum of money to replace our stolen equipment, but *The Village Voice* wrote a big story and we got our first piece in *The New York Times*. Somehow, this awful moment turned into a positive, inspiring one. For me, it was a moral inflection point: Since then, I've never bought anything stolen. In fact, if I find a twenty-dollar bill, I try to find the owner right away. If I can't, I'll give it to charity. Nothing comes for free in this life. There's always a karmic consequence.

Another irony: Had I waited a few months, I would have been flush enough to buy a brand-new DAT machine. A&M Records got so excited about our college radio series that it gave us a $75,000 advance to produce four records under the name, *Live at the Knitting Factory*.

This was a big deal. Hal Willner, the *Saturday Night Live* producer—and one of the first industry players to appreciate what we were doing at The Knit—had introduced me to Steve Ralbovsky, then head of artists and repertoire for A&M.

Inspired by what Elektra had done by signing artists like Zorn and Frisell to its Nonesuch Label, A&M also wanted to release records by innovative artists outside of the mainstream.

When my meeting with Steve started, I was incredibly nervous. A&M was a big label, having signed Janet Jackson, the Police, the Go-Go's, and Bryan Adams. I'd sent Swamp Thing's demo tape to Steve but could never get a return call. Now, here we were, casually throwing ideas around. Steve said he loved the *Live at the Knitting Factory* concept, and soon we had a deal that allowed us to build a new digital recording studio in the club, fully equipped with a new DAT machine. Each record would feature ten artists who would get tremendous exposure—driving more fans to their shows—and the chance to be signed by A&M.

By then, the family living upstairs had become fed up with the noise and moved out, so our landlord forced us to rent the upstairs apartment. That stretched us financially, but gave us an office for Flaming Pie Records, a dressing room for the musicians and, finally, a real bedroom for me. No more sleeping under the desk! We also put the recording studio up there and split the signal, so Bob could mix the sound for the ears of the customers downstairs differently than for the people listening to the records. (And, if the band didn't like the live recording, it could come back the next day and do it all over.)

A&M released Volumes 1 through 4 of *Live at the Knitting Factory* between May of 1989 and June of 1990. The critics loved it. "It's like opening a few aural windows into the atmospheric tumult of New York's music mix," wrote *Downbeat*. *Musician* magazine called me "a Che Guevara for the sort of risky, courageous modern music" showcased by The Knit: "Yo Michael, viva la revolución!"

Unfortunately, sales of the records—which would have been decent for an independent label—were a disappointment for a big company like A&M. (One senior executive called us their "Special Olympics project.") And, halfway through our release schedule, A&M was acquired by Polygram Records, which had little interest in non-commercial avant-garde music. That, combined with a souring economy, eliminated whatever in-house enthusiasm remained for our series. None of the musicians were offered contracts.

Still, the whole experience was a boon for us. Besides the priceless marketing it generated, the series accelerated our move to digital. With CD sales now surpassing vinyl nationwide, our early adoption of the DAT recorder made the transition a breeze: Not having to transfer the tracks to digital formats made it a simple matter for A&M to release volumes 3 and 4 on CD as well as vinyl.

Also, importantly, the deal allowed us to expand beyond the borders of the United States when I managed to buy the international rights back from A&M. It was not cheap—costing almost half the $75,000 the label had advanced us—but the move gave us direct control of our digital future.

Our global expansion had begun almost by accident, made possible by our entry into the music festival business a couple of years earlier. In the summer of 1988, I figured that if we called our shows a "festival"—especially at the same time the big JVC Jazz Festival was taking place—we could attract far more attention. It worked. Our first festival helped us snag a sponsor, generated lots of favorable press as an alternative to the ho-hum mainstream JVC event, and led to invitations to bring our festivals to Europe.

Our big break was having our first New York festival featured in a long, flattering article in the Dutch publication *de Volkskrant*. Nanette Reese, a programmer at a government-sponsored art center in Holland, saw that piece and called to ask if we could work together to put on an event she called a "Jazz Marathon."

I was excited, but there was one problem: The contract had to be signed immediately and we were so broke that we didn't have one of those fancy new fax machines. Too embarrassed to tell her that, I began improvising madly. "I'll tell you what," I said. "Why don't you wire me $500 to talk about this and we'll get into details later." Surprisingly, Nanette sent the money right away. I ran out and bought a fax machine, we signed the contracts, and the festival was a hit. Just like that, we had broken into the international music scene.

It was astonishing to see how much more receptive Europe and Japan were to our brand of music. These countries worshiped American jazz and avant-garde artists and had large government budgets to fly musicians in, put them up in fancy hotels, and program concerts in magnificent opera houses. (European musicians like the great Dutch composer and orchestra leader Willem Breuker, by contrast, would grumble that, when they visited the US, our lack of government arts support meant they had to play in dingy, cramped dives with the pungent odor of the bathrooms wafting over the stage.)

Inspired by our success in Holland, I thought: *Why not do a whole European tour?* Using contacts offered by

Knitting Factory musicians who had played on the continent, I assembled a tour of twenty-four cities in six weeks during the spring of 1990. Six groups were featured—Sonny Sharrock, The Jazz Passengers, Curlew, the Myra Melford Trio, Miracle Room, and Bosho—with three bands per night performing in two-night festivals. We had two tour buses crisscrossing and leapfrogging each other across thirteen countries—including France, Italy, England, Spain, Germany, Austria, and Holland—with concerts taking place in two different cities each night.

Logistically, it was a challenge. Financially, it was a disaster. In a serious lapse of judgment, I trusted a first-time agent in Belgium to book some of the gigs. In Helsingborg, Sweden, he arranged for the bands to play for the door cover charge, which brought in almost nothing, while we scrambled to pay $800 a night in hotel bills. And, when organizing a concert in East Berlin just before the wall came down, I got shafted by the fluctuating exchange rates of the East and West German marks. All together, the tour lost $30,000. That really hurt. It took us months of tea and beer sales at the Knitting Factory to pay off my maxed-out credit cards, but the experience was a success in another way. Beyond the tremendous publicity—more than a hundred favorable reviews and articles—the tour created a large, ongoing market for our *Live at the Knitting Factory* CDs, which we sold through a German distributor.

Japan was also passionate about our music, with features in jazz magazines and television shows leading to Japanese tourists coming to our shows in New York. A big breakthrough came when the Japanese composer and guitarist

Seigen Ono introduced us to a record label called Tokuma Japan Communications. The company offered us $5,000 per record for ten albums—the four-volume A&M series, plus six more of individual artists performing live at the Knitting Factory. That created crucial cash flow, allowing me to offer artists like The Jazz Passengers and the multi-instrumentalist Thomas Chapin $5,000 to record their gigs, which they readily accepted, for release on our label, Knitting Factory Records. Since we retained the right to sell the music outside of Japan, we'd make our money marketing CDs to their fans in Europe.

Oddly enough, it was the sheer portability of CDs that made our transition to digital profitable. In the early '90s, I organized an event in Frankfurt on summer weekends and found that I could stuff 200 CDs into two army duffel bags, bring them on my flight, and sell them at shows. Vinyl LPs would have taken up a lot more room and the baggage handlers would have surely smashed them to bits in transit. In those days, a round-trip flight from New York to Frankfurt cost just $275 on Lufthansa and you could check two bags for free. The CDs themselves only cost about two dollars each to make—and that dropped in half as the format caught on—so the profit margin was excellent.

When Chapin's Trio appeared in Frankfurt, for example, he would kill it on stage and his pumped-up fans would snatch up all 200 CDs at about twenty dollar each in US dollars. Every weekend, for most of the summer—a different artist appearing each week—I'd fly out on a Friday night and return Sunday with an empty duffel bag and over $4,000 in cash (far more than we ever sold in stores through our American distributor).

It reminded me of my teenage years at the Seven Mile Fair, when business was so simple and fun, like running a lemonade stand. You set up a table and hand over a physical product for cash. This was business at its most satisfying: Fans flocking to my table, excited to buy a high-quality product. Those sales helped the Knitting Factory brand grow, expanded our relationships throughout Europe, and helped our cash flow become a little more predictable.

With the Knitting Factory club still a break-even proposition at best, these trips not only brought home badly needed revenue, but reversed our business model to something more like the classic music-industry arrangement of the time—our live shows serving mostly to promote our more profitable arm, Knitting Factory Records. Despite the rave reviews our club was getting as the exciting new center of the downtown scene, we were still living hand-to-mouth, partly because our rent kept going up as we grew. Not long after taking over the upstairs apartment, we expanded downstairs as well, into Estella's Peruvian Cafe on the first floor. That was triggered more by aesthetic considerations than business ones: John Zorn wanted to present the world premiere of his new band, Naked City, in the spring of 1989, when our main stage was already booked. It was a typical Zorn enterprise—extremely ambitious and more than a little out there—but he was such a musical giant, I *had* to find a space for his band to play.

At the time, nobody knew that Naked City, with its lineup of phenomenal musicians—Bill Frisell (guitar), Fred Frith (bass), Wayne Horvitz (keyboards), Joey Baron (drums) and Zorn (sax)—would become so influential in the avant-garde world. They played an often raucous and loud mashup of jazz, surf, progressive rock, classical, heavy metal, country, punk rock, and God knows what else. All I knew was that we needed Estella to rent us her place for five nights in May. When she tried to gouge us by demanding $1,000 a night—her rent was only $3,000 a month!—I realized it made more sense to just buy out her lease altogether. We had to buy all her kitchen equipment too, making the deal quite expensive, but it included her full liquor license. That would finally allow us to sell high-margin spirits in addition to the usual wine and beer. (We'd wanted to do this for years, but only one full liquor license was allowed per building.)

While the financial rationale for this expansion was dubious, the artistic result was fantastic. Zorn and his crew put on a spectacular show—rehearsing twenty-five new compositions during the day and then performing them at night, a cycle they repeated for five straight nights, adding new material each time. That gave Naked City an enormous repertoire for a long tour of Europe and a series of seminal recordings over several years. Those concerts were a magical time that really defined the early Knit—the music drove everything and, even though the place was packed, we hardly sold any drinks. I didn't care about the lost revenue. At that moment, all that mattered was the musical genius pouring from this amazing composer who was clearly creating a once-in-a-lifetime experience.

Looking back on those days, I don't know how we survived. Sometimes, we couldn't even pay the electrical bill, which could run $2,000 a month. One afternoon, a Con Ed rep showed up saying he wanted to check the meters. Once he got inside, he secretly shut off the power and then scampered away. We only made it through the shows that night by running extension cords from our office upstairs, which had a separate residential account. (Our idea of revenge was printing "Fuck Con Edison" across our calendar for November and December of 1990.) Things were so dire, in fact, that, when two polite gentlemen in fine Italian suits paid us a visit one night, these upstanding members of the local crime family saw so little money coming into our cash registers that they decided extortion wasn't even worth the trouble—beyond, that is, the mob-owned sanitation service we'd already hired to pick up our garbage to avoid retribution. "We're all good," one of the men said with a wink as they got up from the bar and walked out. If I wasn't so relieved, I would have been deeply insulted.

We tried all sorts of schemes to hustle a buck—self-publishing a magazine called *Knitting Factory Knotes*, a book about the club's origins called *Knitting Music*, and a tour of the West Coast in the spring of 1991. The publications proved to be a cash sinkhole and the tour turned a small profit only thanks to the sales of T-shirts and CDs. We even opened an office in Amsterdam staffed by my brother Josh, who was living there at the time, to book festivals in Europe and sell CDs, but every project was hit-or-miss. With no stability in sight, the whole scene got to be too much for Bob. I didn't blame him a bit when he left in early 1992 to work as an independent music producer.

All this craziness wasn't easy for me, either, but I loved it—both the rewards *and* the risks. I loved dreaming up new schemes to solve whatever problem cropped up, and it was fun not knowing what the next day would bring. I was also hugely grateful to be at the center of this incredibly vibrant artistic scene that I had stumbled into. Plus, I wasn't alone in this adventure: In October of 1991, I got married.

I'd met Sarah Connors at Washington University in St. Louis a decade earlier when she was a freshman and I was a sophomore. I was president of the Outing Club—I've always had a passion for spelunking, rock climbing, backpacking and canoeing (still do!)—and was sitting behind a table in the quad one day, trying to sign people up, when a cute girl with a lovely dancer's body came walking by. There was something special about her. I liked everything about her! I convinced Sarah to join the club and later ran into her at a party. By then, I was smitten. I got her dorm-room number and showed up the next day with a card and flowers to ask her on a date to an art museum.

Sarah and I dated throughout college—breaking up every few months and then getting back together—and we continued to see each other from time to time, even after I went to Spain for a year and she finished college and started film school at New York University. In fact, she was a big reason I dropped out of law school in 1986 and moved to Manhattan to become a music mogul.

Committed relationships are tough when you're young, so we remained on-and-off for the first few years after the Knitting Factory opened. I finally achieved some domestic stability in 1989, when I bought my own apartment on Mott Street, a stone's throw from the club. It was a cute studio with a small courtyard that cost $90,000. (My parents helped me with the down payment and it turned out to be a great investment when we sold it a few years later for $150,000.) Sarah began spending more and more time there and, at some point, we looked at each other and said, "Are we going to keep fooling around or do we want to, you know, get serious?" That was the moment of truth. So, in 1990, I asked this creative, kind, insightful woman to marry me. Sarah moved in, and soon, we were looking for spots for a wedding in the beautiful Hudson Valley of upstate New York.

One day, while rock climbing near New Paltz with my college friend George Gatch, I found the perfect place. The catch was we'd have to buy the property—a dilapidated house with a big backyard lawn, surrounded by woods, that backed up on the mountains. The price: $142,000. George split the $20,000 down payment with me and Sarah (our half was a wedding gift from my parents) and we bought the place together. Some friends helped whitewash the decrepit house, an all-star klezmer band drove up from the city, and the wedding was an amazing day to remember. Sarah and I still own the original house—George and I have each built homes on the property further up the mountain—and City Winery had its first company off-site meeting there in 2009. Over the years, this beautiful property has become an invaluable place for reflection, hiking, and recharging.

Finally, at the age of twenty-nine, I was settling down, but life at the Knitting Factory was as frenetic as ever. After taking over three floors of 47 E. Houston Street, I still wanted more space, ideally in a building that was not only bigger and better, but also *safer*. I'm a builder, always have been, and there's nothing I love more than getting my hands dirty with a renovation project—demolishing walls, adding doors and windows, wiring electricity—but, at the Knitting Factory, these projects were usually done on the fly, and may not have been, shall we say, entirely up to code. In those days, building inspections were lax, and I had trouble sleeping at night worrying that a floor might collapse, or a fire would break out while we had a full house, creating a stampede.

After some hunting, I found a spot at 74 Leonard Street in Tribeca, about a mile south of the original location. At 10,500 square feet on three floors, it had twice as much space, bigger rooms, and, as part of a historical district, was much classier than our old dump. The basics of a club or restaurant were already there. The ground floor had a bar/cafe in the front. There was a larger performance space with a balcony and, with an occupancy of 299, it was officially three times as big as the old club. We demolished the kitchen to create a dressing room. We also created a "tap bar" offering craft beer and a performance area we called the "Alterknit Theater." The lowest level, a basement, had room for an office and a recording studio.

The rent was not cheap—at $10,000 a month, it was five times more than we had been paying—and I had to take out a $400,000 loan to pay for renovations and equipment (thanks for co-signing, Dad!). But the move in March of 1994 was well worth it. Now we had excellent exits to the streets in case of emergency, a legitimate fire-alarm system, and professional contractors to do the necessary work. We were awarded legal public-assembly permits and never went over our occupancy limit (well, almost never). At a time when there had been a number of nightclub fires in the city, *The Village*

Voice called us "New York's safest club." Finally, I was able to sleep at night.

Our new club was also much more high tech, since there was so much buzz about something called the Information Superhighway that was about to change the world. In the front hallway, as customers walked in, they encountered a fat Mac desktop computer that they could use to surf this newfangled thing called the World Wide Web.

While upgrading the recording studio, I began fantasizing about buying a new piece of tech that was blowing my mind. The transformation from atoms to bits that Nicholas Negroponte had predicted seemed to be finally happening. I was reading in *Wired* magazine and other places that music could now be distributed not only on clunky CDs but with computers, as digital files, over the internet.

At that moment, a light bulb went off. Before my trips to Frankfurt, I had been struggling with how many music CDs to order. The CD-pressing company required minimum orders of 2,500, making it hard to manage so much inventory—and predict how many copies a particular artist would sell. By then, I had dabbled in using the web to take orders for CDs and mailing them to customers. But sending the actual product itself over the internet? That seemed impossible, like the stuff of science fiction. But, if true, it could be a tremendous business opportunity.

This was still five years before Napster would upend the music industry by allowing users to freely share MP3 files, and seven years before Steve Jobs and Apple would release iTunes and the iPod. Nobody knew precisely how this so-called Digital Revolution would play out. As a club owner, I began to wonder how the internet might transform the idea of a live show when fans might no longer have to be physically present to enjoy it.

Then I learned that a California company called Xing Technologies (pronounced "Zing") had developed the first software program that allowed users to stream audio and video over the internet. I was ecstatic. I had to have a *Xing* box. Of course, I didn't *really* need this device to run my business any more than I needed a DAT machine when it came out seven years earlier. But being an early adopter had greatly helped my recording business make the transition to CDs—directly boosting our bottom line—so who knows what fantastic future I might be creating by having one of these magic boxes?

Xing servers were not easy to come by, even though internet connections in those days were so slow that streaming video was incredibly frustrating to watch, coming out all herky-jerky. One industry, in particular, was buying them up as fast as they could be stamped out—and it wasn't sports, academia, or mainstream entertainment. Turns out the porn business was snatching up all the available Xing Boxes to stream live sex shows, making it nearly impossible for anybody else to get his hands on one.

Finally, one Friday, I found a dealer who agreed to bring me one of these precious boxes on Sunday morning—$2,750 in cash, no haggling. That was a lot of money for me. The only way I could afford it was to siphon off our sales receipts that weekend. So I watched our bars closely on Friday and Saturday nights, hoping enough free-spending customers would arrive so there would be enough dough left over after I paid the staff.

Fortunately, just enough business materialized, and I stuffed the cash into an envelope. It felt like a seedy drug deal: The mysterious guy showed up at the club door at 9 a.m. and I gave him the envelope. He counted the cash and handed me the box. Then he disappeared, without even offering advice about how to hook the damn thing up.

At last, I owned the key to a bright digital future. It was an amazing time to be alive: Time and space were being obliterated now that the most profound human experiences could be transmitted around the planet instantly. Like a kid on an acid trip, I began to imagine the walls of our club becoming porous, melting away, as our community was embraced by people around the globe, all day and every night.

In truth, I had no idea what I was messing with. All I knew was that my experiments with technology so far had given me a nice buzz: Business was growing at a healthy pace and life was good. Little did I know that, as endless possibilities unfolded before me, I was about to cross a line that would lead me to ruin.

3

Keep It Real

Why do companies with promising technology fail? It's not necessarily because their ideas are bad. Some of the most spectacular flame-outs of the dot-com era—Webvan (groceries), Pets.com (pet supplies), Boo.com (apparel), and Wine.com—were followed decades later by entrepreneurs who found success mining the very same territory.

While some of those startups imploded because they were too early to market, or executed badly, the biggest flaw of many entrepreneurs is seeing technology as a magic potion that makes them exempt from the laws of nature. This mindset remains surprisingly common today, given the absurd valuations of some tech firms that are still not turning a profit.

The trouble often starts when a company has some success—attracting venture capital, customers, online traffic, positive press, maybe launching an IPO—and, in the rush of excitement, commits the cardinal sin of failing to Keep It Real.

By that, I simply mean not paying attention to critical business fundamentals.

That probably sounds like a dumb-ass mistake that should be easy to avoid. Well, let me tell you a story.

I'm not blaming the Xing box. Honestly. It was a fine video-streaming machine that did the job well (at least for its time). But, if technology is like fine wine, the benefits clearly begin to dissipate when we overindulge. Our perceptions become impaired, our judgment clouded. We become like the partygoer who fails to see a problem with stripping to our underwear, dancing the conga with a lampshade on our head, and then wondering why everyone else is heading for the door!

My first few experiments as an early adopter were as productive as they were exciting: recording shows with our new digital-tape machine, moving from pressing vinyl to CDs, communicating with customers via electronic mail. So the Xing box I bought in 1994 seemed like a natural next step. It wasn't—any more than doing shots of 180-proof moonshine is a good idea after a luscious bottle of Chateau Petrus from Bordeaux. Because suddenly having the ability to stream our concerts around the world began to give me the craziest ideas.

By then, I was thirty-two and had fully embraced the new digital lifestyle, reading *Wired* magazine since its first issue and adopting the digerati's new lingo and precocious attitude: *Man, if you can't grok compression algorithms, you're obviously a newbie—but try to wrap your mind around the fact that we're going through the biggest phreaking revolution since Gutenberg's printing press!* When I got around to programming music for the summer of 1995—and needing more revenue to cover the $10,000 monthly rent of our new Tribeca location—I thought: *Why not try to stream it worldwide?*

Like other New York club owners, I was desperate to fill the void left by the recent demise of the New Music Seminar. This annual festival and conference for new rock bands had been a cash cow for fifteen years, bringing large crowds of attendees wearing conference badges who would club-hop and drink like fish. I went to some fellow small-club owners and Andrew Rasiej of Irving Plaza, one of the bigger venues in town, to see if they wanted to help me launch my crazy idea: a music festival streamed all over the world. Andrew said, "Great idea," but wondered who our sponsor would be.

I didn't have one, so I got in touch with a sponsorship broker, Stuart Racey, who connected me to Apple Computer. In those pre-iTunes days, Apple had just started exploring the music space and David Pakman, the twenty-six-year-old co-founder of the Apple Music Group (who also was a musician), sounded intrigued. So I wrote up a proposal and he agreed to pony up $75,000 to make Apple our main sponsor. RealNetworks also became a sponsor when its founder Rob Glaser approached me, insisting that I use his newfangled server instead of the Xing box. I was reluctant—after all the trouble I went through wresting that thing away from the porn industry!—but I finally agreed and brought his company on board too.

Our Macintosh New York Music Festival, or "Mac Fest," made history as the first major American music festival to stream its concerts online. Musicians came out of the woodwork to participate. When it opened in July of 1995 at fifteen venues across the city, we had 350 bands, including Todd Rundgren and the Residents. At each location, festival goers gathered around Macintosh computers we had set up to display the live video stream, giving the events a hip, futuristic feel. Hyping the event, I told *The New York Times*, "This festival will be looked at in twenty-five years as the moment when ancient forms of musical communication and the future of media collided." To drive the point home, I started our daytime Plug In Conference of music-industry folks by dramatically blowing into a shofar, a ram's horn used at Jewish New Year ceremonies, to announce that we stood at an epochal moment in history. As a further provocation, I started one of our panel discussions by asking the assembled heavyweights from the major record labels, "Aren't you afraid that you all will soon be out of jobs?"

In retrospect, my behavior was a bit hucksterish, even juvenile—no doubt irritating to the record-industry people who had every reason to fear for their jobs. Nevertheless, I sincerely believed what I was saying and figured that, at the very least, it would be great for business, which it was. The laugh was on us, however, at least temporarily, because the commercial internet was still in its infancy. The World Wide Web had been invented only five years earlier by the British scientist Tim Berners-Lee (we double fact-checked that, as I thought Al Gore invented it). By then, only 5 percent of American households were online, mostly with painfully slow

14.4-baud modems over phone lines using services like AOL, CompuServe, and Prodigy. The festival's infrastructure was also sorely lacking. Some clubs didn't have enough phone lines to make the webcasts work. Fuses blew at venues with faulty electrical wiring and beer spills short-circuited gear. Equipment was stolen or vandalized.

The Knitting Factory didn't have nearly as many problems because we were properly wired with a high-bandwidth T-1 line. And, when we got an email from fans in Singapore saying they were watching the show, we practically hit the roof. Then came a note from Paris, causing more cheers to break out. We only reached a few thousand people online that year, and the images were herky-jerky at best, but the potential was clear and overwhelming. As a record guy, I knew how hard it was to get a single person to pay for a CD or vinyl LP. Now we could reach millions with the click of a button!

Napster was still four years away from revolutionizing the music industry, but college students had already begun illegally swapping MP3 files over the Internet and the value of content was starting to change. In those days, even a 28.8-baud modem took two hours to download a thirty-six-minute CD. It seemed clear that legal services would eventually appear as bandwidth increased, so my plan was to make live-streaming shows at the Knitting Factory the free taster; eventually, fans would pay to download singles or even entire albums.

For the music industry, one big obstacle was working out the intellectual property rights, but I had already sorted that out with our Knitting Factory artists. I gave each one

$5,000 to record a particular concert; in return, they gave me the rights to sell the music via CD or any other medium, usually with an industry standard of 15 percent going to the artist for the master recording itself and 50 percent for the publishing rights (which included radio airplay, film/TV use, and mechanical royalties, though none of these usually amounted to much for our jazz and avant-garde musicians). When our record company was done selling the music, our agreements allowed for all rights to revert to the artist.

Though I hyped the potential of internet music every chance I got, in private moments, I still wondered how profitable it would become. Remembering the simplicity of the Seven Mile Fair of my youth, I wished I had a physical product to sell and a clear understanding of where my profits would be coming from. I kept saying, "This World Wide Web thing is exciting, but I still wish I could find a way to sell those people drinks. How can we digitize beer?"

The internet, however, was not about immediate or even near-term profits. It was about a glorious future, one that seemed just out of reach. At the time, industry analysts were making wild predictions about the hundreds of millions of broadband users who would soon be online. That made everybody want a piece of the action, driven by a constant fear of being left behind.

One person who helped keep my feet on the ground in those days was Lou Reed. We had met while our new Leonard Street club was under construction. Hal Willner, the same producer who had earlier connected me to A&M Records, brought Lou by one day while I was covered in sawdust building the box office. As we shook hands, I was awe-struck, having been a huge fan since high school when we all listened to his Velvet Underground records and the famous *Lou Reed Live* album with songs like "Vicious" and "Walk on the Wild Side." To me, Lou Reed was the ultimate New York musician, but we always considered him too big and famous to play at the Knitting Factory. Now here I was, looking like a construction worker and nervously showing him where we were putting the dressing room and recording studio. He had a lot of questions and suggestions about the sound—the stage, the acoustics, the PA system—because, to him, performing was never about the scene or the fame. It was always about the music. It's hard to put into words why that short, twenty-minute walk-through had such an impact, but it felt like our new club was receiving a kind of blessing from the God of Downtown New York rock.

After opening, I was able to use that connection to book a few nights with Lou, a dream come true. That brought substantial crowds and press and started a string of three-night runs over the next few years. Lou and I also developed a profound relationship around Judaism. (He once said that, although he was Jewish, his real God was rock 'n' roll.) In 1994, I started an annual Passover seder event at the club and, in the second year, I invited him. Each artist in attendance took a small role in telling the Passover story and Lou, fittingly, was the "wise child." (John Zorn was the "bad child.") Lou's reading was relaxed and heartfelt, and his delivery with twinkling eyes gave me a sense of the depths of his soul. I rarely saw the hard exterior shell—tough, mean, and menacing—for which he was well known. In ways he was probably unaware of, his honest approach to everything he did, and his rejection of all the music industry bullshit, was a true inspiration.

By 1996, bullshit was in copious supply as the new internet economy gathered steam. At this point, it was hard not to let things go to my head. Though the Knitting Factory was still barely breaking even, to the outside world, it looked like everything I touched was turning to gold. Our annual summer music festival–"What Is Jazz?"–was kicking the *tuchus* of George Wein's venerable JVC Jazz Festival, offering more concerts, more artists, and a much wider variety of music. In fact, I decided to run our festival at exactly the same time as Wein's to directly challenge his hegemony. "Every year the What Is Jazz? Festival has taken on weight," wrote the music critic Peter Watrous in *The New York Times*, "while the JVC Jazz Festival has become increasingly irrelevant."

Meanwhile, *New York* magazine named me one of their top ten New Yorkers of 1996–along with Derek Jeter and Natalie Portman!–and had me dress up in a backward beret and a fine suit for rakish photos. The story called me "the kind of wizard who can make futuristic jazz both marketable and global–call him the impresario of the downtown music scene." The gala dinner the magazine threw to promote the Top Ten issue was a blast. For a while, I felt famous.

To top it off, music industry titan Larry Rosen appeared out of nowhere to request a meeting to ask me for advice. I couldn't believe it. After making a fortune leading the vinyl-to-CD revolution with his independent GRP label, Rosen now wanted to spearhead the transition to online music with his new company, N2K. He'd gotten funding from David Bowie and the Rolling Stones and hired Phil Ramone, one of the greatest music producers of all time, but he still had a million questions. Since I'd been experimenting with this stuff for two years, he wanted to know everything: How I managed webcasting, recorded live shows, sold mail-order CDs via the web, planned to offer digital downloads, the whole shebang. What an ego boost!

My latest venture, I told Larry, was hooking up with Andrew Rasiej, my partner in Mac Fest, to create a new company called the Digital Club Network with a business plan I'd written over a long weekend. Member clubs around the country and, eventually, around the world, would webcast live shows and archive them for sale in the future. Most of the bands were unknown, of course, but our hope was that early recordings of the next Bruce Springsteen or Pearl Jam would end up becoming very valuable, indeed.

Being in the middle of all this action improved my social life too. I hung out with my Tribeca neighbor Jaron Lanier, the dreadlocked pioneer of virtual reality who is also an accomplished composer and writer. I began organizing dinners at the big loft apartment Sarah and I were renting and invited industry heavyweights like Rosen and Pakman. This allowed me to hold forth about my new passion, fine wine, and my favorite French Hermitages and Montrachets. Looking back, I cringe at the pretentiousness of these "Wine and Technology" dinners, but the guests seemed to love them.

Around this time, I brought in my first outside investors—smart, seasoned pros named Cy Leslie and Bob Linton, who wanted to explore the online music space. Cy was the founder of Pickwick Records (where Lou Reed used to work as a staff songwriter, coincidentally) and he had formed an investment firm with Bob, the former CEO of Drexel Burnham Lambert. Being new to the online scene, Cy and Bob wanted to emphasize business basics, which I was glad to hear—a welcome relief from the internet hype. They wanted us to become more professional—buy non-Mac computers with accounting software, keep better track of money, and hire lawyers to set up the company properly. Most importantly, I took their advice to form a board of directors to meet every quarter to offer advice on our growth.

I agreed with all that, but I also wanted to use some of the money to establish a new umbrella company, "Knit Media," to help us grow. I knew we could be so much more than a nightclub (or, eventually, a chain of clubs), a record company, and a festival producer. Now was our chance to become a full-fledged media company with a worldwide reach that could include websites, television projects, film, print publications, and whatever else we could dream up. Cy and Bob liked the sound of that, and really believed in me. After some back and forth, they agreed in 1996 to provide $500,000 in capital in exchange for 10 percent of the company.

I was ecstatic. My little company was now valued at $5 million, making my stake worth $4.5 million! I was rich—at least on paper. On a more practical level, I would finally get a regular paycheck. Ever since the Knitting Factory opened nine years before, I paid myself only after settling with our landlord, vendors, and employees. Fortunately, Sarah was doing well as a freelance film producer and was able to support us during lean times. Now, at the ripe age of thirty-four, I was finally collecting a check every Friday. It wasn't a big check, but it was enough that Sarah and I could relax a bit.

Feeling flush, I pushed ahead with our third annual cyber festival, now sponsored by Intel, a sweet deal that Andrew landed. Apple, roiled by turmoil before Steve Jobs returned as CEO, had withdrawn its sponsorship and Intel was busy trying to beat Apple at the music game. So, for four days in July of 1997, the Intel New York Music Festival became our biggest and best to date, with 400 bands in twenty clubs and another 150 acts streaming concerts from outside the city. With far more corporate resources and wider bandwidth, the technology worked much better this time, attracting 100,000 online viewers, ten times greater than the year before. "The video, at six frames per second, had a herky-jerky look to it," wrote Forbes, pointing out that even the first moon landing, nearly thirty years ago and hundreds of thousands of miles away, had a better picture. We didn't mind. We knew those images would improve as bandwidth continued to increase.

Besides, more investors were showing up at our doors and, in 1997, we took on another partner. Unlike Cy and Bob, this internet investment group didn't talk much about business fundamentals; they were clearly just hoping to cash in quickly as the dot-com craze gained momentum. This was my first indication of how wild things were getting. For $500,000, we gave this group 5 percent of the company, half of what Cy and Bob got for the same amount less than a year earlier. That instantly doubled the company's valuation to $10 million and pushed my stake to $9 million! Yikes!

With that capital, we expanded to 3,000 square feet of new office space on Worth Street, one block away from the Knitting Factory, and Knit Media had an extremely prolific year: We replaced our annual What Is Jazz? festival with a bigger event, the Texaco New York Jazz Festival. With the oil giant Texaco as our new sponsor, we presented 300 performances over two weeks in June featuring Don Was, Ginger Baker, Pharoah Sanders and the Art Ensemble of Chicago, as well as Knitting Factory regulars like Bill Frisell. It was "probably the most extensive avant-garde festival in the United States," raved the *Chicago Tribune*. Meanwhile, we were still doing tours in Europe and doing a brisk business selling CDs there.

We also got into television, in a backward way. After a few years of webcasting, we realized that a single camera showing a concert is boring. I contacted my friend Mitch Goldman, who was making some music television shows, and asked him to join us. We went out and bought a bunch of new cameras but discovered that hiring four camera operators and an editor was hugely expensive—$600 to $800 for each show that attracted only a few clicks and produced no revenue. But the music and video quality were so good, I thought: *Why not sell it to television?* So we did, the result being the Black Entertainment Television's (BET) *Live from the Knitting Factory* series that ran for three seasons. Instead of old media getting into new media, we were doing it ass-backwards—an internet venture that needed an old-fashioned cable network to make it work. BET gave us advance money and priceless exposure, and the network got lots of prestige content: seminal concerts by Lou Reed, John Zorn, Charles Lloyd, Cecil Taylor, and others, with BET paying all the publishing and royalties directly to the artists.

Amid all this activity, I sometimes stepped back and marveled at how far the Knitting Factory had come from our humble roots as a small cafe started by a couple of knuckleheads from Wisconsin. Something about that contrast bothered me, but I couldn't quite put my finger on it until the day Zorn exploded at me.

The legendary composer was doing his preshow ritual, rehearsing new material for the show that night, when someone accidentally left our webcasting machinery running. Like most artists, Zorn would never allow such private moments to be broadcast without his permission, not to mention financial compensation. Later, we found out it was an honest mistake by a staffer, but some of that music did get streamed to anyone on the planet who happened to be visiting our site.

Enraged, Zorn went off on me, right in front of the stage. The precise language has been lost to time, but imagine the most coarse and creative ways to say, "Go fuck yourself, you greedy motherfucker!" Really tore me a new one. Nobody was trying to steal his magnificent work, but, in retrospect, I can see that I had it coming. By then, I had become sloppy and lost sight of what was important: the music and the dignity of the artists making it. I wasn't hanging around to enjoy the shows anymore. I was so caught up in the technology, cutting deals, getting media attention, selling drinks—calling it *content*, not *music*—that I wasn't paying enough attention to the needs of the artists. Or my hard-working employees, for that matter. What a schmuck!

That moment hurt because, in many ways, Zorn was the embodiment of the original Knitting Factory vibe. From our earliest days, he kind of adopted us, and he always felt a great obligation to the whole New York avant-garde scene to make sure we took good care of the artists: that the deals were straight, the sound was good, and there was lots of high-quality water in the dressing room (a particular fixation of his). Zorn taught me a lot, and I listened to him carefully because I really wanted the Knitting Factory to feel like a welcoming home for all of our musicians.

It's hard to know what the last straw was for Zorn, but it may have started the night in May of 1997 when Lou Reed called me up and said, "Hey, my friend Vaclav Havel is coming to town and we're thinking about going to the Knitting Factory. What have you got?"

Excited but trying to act casual, I said, "Oh, it's Zorn doing the music of Masada." That was both the name of Zorn's band and his fabulous collection of short compositions rooted in his Jewish heritage. "Wow, Vaclav would love that," Lou said, and suggested the Czech president and his security guards sit in the balcony upstairs. "Can you put out a little nosh, some wine? It will be very chill," he assured me.

"Of course," I said. I'd do anything for Lou.

On the day of the show, Lou called again and said the secretary of state would like to join us if that was okay. "Madeleine Albright?" I stammered. "Um, sure, no problem."

The next thing I knew, Secret Service agents flooded into the club and the NYPD wanted to block off the whole street.

That night, Zorn started the show right on time, as always. I was in the balcony with Lou and Havel, watching intently. It was an all-acoustic concert, so the sound system had been turned off, and a hush had fallen over the crowd. Nobody wanted to miss a single note. Zorn on his sax started off with a beautiful, intense piece with Dave Douglas on trumpet, Greg Cohen on double bass, and Joey Baron on drums.

Suddenly, there was a commotion behind us. The balcony door opened, and the secretary of state strode in with some other dignitaries and about twenty Secret Service agents and guards wearing earpieces and talking into their wrists. Madam Secretary greeted President Havel and they started talking. Lou was introduced, and I got a quick handshake. Their assistants started talking to one another, yakking it up, and suddenly everybody was making a racket.

The music stopped. Zorn looked up. "Hey, you upstairs, shut the fuck up!"

The agents immediately reached for their belts, scanning the scene for danger. Havel and Albright looked terribly embarrassed and murmured apologies. Lou and I, huddled in the corner, looked at each other and tried to keep from bursting out laughing. Finally, everybody quieted down, and Zorn started the music again.

At the time, Zorn had no clue who was causing the ruckus. If he had, he probably would have shouted twice as loud. If you're not being respectful of the music, he doesn't care who you are—you need to shut the fuck up. To me, the incident was nothing but a bizarre, funny confluence of circumstances that would never happen again. Not to Zorn. After he screamed at me for the sound-check privacy violation and chewed out Madeleine Albright, I couldn't escape the feeling that our Patron Saint of the Avant-garde now saw the Knitting Factory as a duplicitous, greedy place where special treatment for famous people had become more important than the music—which, for him, was nothing less than a sacred calling. He was right. Zorn's outburst at the event made *Rolling Stone* magazine and remains one of my craziest memories, a definite inflection point.

The following year, Zorn was gone. He took his boundless creativity to a new club called Tonic, a former kosher winery on the Lower East Side that reminded me of the Knitting Factory when we started. With cheap rent, lousy plumbing, and building-code violations, it became Zorn's new hangout and a popular new gathering place for downtown musicians. I was sad to see John go—I treasured his music and his friendship—but was happy that he was helping expand the scene and give artists another place to play.

Zorn's departure had a kind of ripple effect on other musicians, who appeared to be increasingly frustrated at the challenges of being a jazz artist in capitalist America when the dot-com boom seemed to be minting new millionaires every day. As the Knit grew into a multimillion-dollar media company, they evidently thought I was one of those nouveau riche bastards exploiting them to line my pockets. That wasn't remotely true. My wealth on paper was speculative, at best, and I always paid the artists as much as I possibly could, but, at certain moments, such perceptions can take on a life of their own.

Things reached a head in the summer of 1998, when Texaco again sponsored our summer jazz festival, this time for $500,000, twice as much as the previous year. Seeing those dollar signs inspired some musicians to picket outside the Knitting Factory, carrying signs and demanding higher wages. They didn't realize that, after covering the costs of staging 350 concerts over two weeks in June, and offering many of the shows for free, our net profit was actually quite small. Many of the protesters were friends of mine, so it was an awkward moment. I went outside to listen to their complaints and agreed to a minimum pay rate at festivals. Satisfied, they called it quits by afternoon. As someone who always considered himself staunchly on the side of the artists, the demonstration hurt. But I had also heard expressions of gratitude from musicians for helping to expand the market for their resolutely noncommercial music. One of the protest organizers, my friend, the guitarist Marc Ribot, told *The New York Times* a few years later that I was "the fairest employer of jazz musicians in New York," adding that the Knitting Factory's pay rates were the best in the city.

Hearing that meant a lot to me, as did the words of George Wein, the legendary jazz-festival producer with whom I'd had a friendly rivalry for years. When I told him musicians I was once so close to were now looking at me suspiciously, like I had some of their money in my pocket, he said, "That means that you finally made it. You're The Man now. And, when you're The Man, people are going to look at you that way. And there is really nothing that you can do about it." Hearing that from someone as revered as George made me feel much better.

At the same time, I can see now that the musicians were probably picking up on ways that I had changed since starting the Knitting Factory eleven years earlier. One thing I've noticed about digital technology is that its tremendous power can make users feel superhuman. And so it was with me. At the age of thirty-six, I was starting to feel like the new King of the Hill of internet music. I was getting so drunk on tech that I was unwittingly barreling over the line from shrewd early adopter to that drunk at the party. Everyone can see he's an idiot—except him.

Ego consumed me first, then money.

As if hanging out with rock stars, foreign presidents, and cabinet secretaries were not enough, one day, out of the blue, I got a call from Quincy Jones. Hard to believe, but the most successful producer in pop-music history, the genius behind Michael Jackson's mega-hit *Thriller* album and *We Are the World*, and winner of a billion Grammy Awards, wanted to ask *me* for advice!

Quincy had just started a website devoted to South African music and was thinking about opening a new internet-connected nightclub called Q's Jook Joint. He wanted to swing by the Knitting Factory to see what we were up to—check out our stage, recording facilities, and internet hookups. He seemed genuinely impressed with our setup and, when the tour was over, he announced that he had made reservations at Nobu, the nearby restaurant run by celebrity chef Nobu Matsuhisa. We could have easily walked but took his limo instead.

There were four in our group—Quincy and I each brought along a financial adviser—and, while we ate dinner and drank sake in tall bamboo carafes, famous people like MTV's then-chief Tom Freston came by to say hello. After dinner, our advisers excused themselves and I was in heaven, left alone with the great Quincy Jones to hear stories about him playing trumpet in Dizzy Gillespie's band and producing Miles Davis's final album at the Montreux Jazz Festival.

After about an hour, and lots of sake, two young men came by. "Yo, Q!" Quincy said, getting up to hug Q-Tip, the famous rapper and producer from A Tribe Called Quest. Meanwhile, the other guy, a white dude, sat down next to me with a smile and said, "Do you think I'm getting a little fat?"

By now, the night was feeling extremely surreal. "I don't know how skinny you were before," I said, "but you look fine to me." He asked me what I did for a living, and I told him that I ran a club down the street and Quincy and I were just rapping about our experiments with the internet. We talked about me and my adventures for quite a while until some people came by the table and said, "Hi, Leo!" Finally, I asked him what he did for a living and he said he was a movie actor. "Oh, been in anything I might have seen?" He said, "Well, Kate Winslet and I recently came out with a film called *Titanic*."

I felt like the biggest ass in the world for not realizing I was talking to Leonardo DiCaprio, star of the highest-grossing film of all time. We laughed about it, had some more sake, and everything was fine. We closed the joint and Leo and Q-Tip asked if the Knitting Factory was open. "Nah," I said, but suddenly got the idea to bring them by our new apartment, right near the club. I wanted to see Sarah's face when I walked through the door with Leonardo DiCaprio and Q-Tip. Quincy got into his limo and drove away as the three of us, young drunken stars, stumbled through the doors of Nobu and rambled up to Leonard Street.

That moment—floating on air from an incredible night out and bringing my famous new friends home—ranked as one of the highlights of my life. But things went downhill quickly from there. Through the sake fog, I remembered that not only was it well after midnight, but Sarah was pregnant with twins due in a few weeks. Maybe charging through the door and waking her up was not a good idea. "That's cool," they said. Then we said our goodbyes on the sidewalk and promised to get together soon to hear music together. After that night, I never saw my pal Leo again (although I have run into Q-Tip and Quincy).

That was disappointing. Man, I thought Leo and I were besties! Fortunately, a much bigger highlight of my life happened a few weeks later, when Eli and Zachary were born. I'd made a quantum leap from the most superficial kind of relationships to the most profound. Five years later, we would have another child, a girl named Sophia, and my wife and three children still form the rock-solid foundation of my life.

Through the sleepless nights of new parenthood, Knit Media continued to grow like crazy. Our annual cyber festival, sponsored by Intel again in 1998, was bigger than ever, with 300 acts in twenty clubs, including Ronnie Spector and a surprise appearance by Debbie Harry. My Digital Club Network with Andrew and a new partner, Ted Werth, was adding dozens of member nightclubs who liked our ideas for monetizing the webcasting of shows: selling the big record labels information about fans of unsigned bands; creating our own label to sign some of those bands before the majors did; offering single pay-per-view concerts or all-you-can-eat subscription packages; selling CDs of concerts to fans on their way out of the club, and much more.

Speculative? Sure, but so was everything about the internet in those days. With my ego swelling rapidly, now it was time for money to do its number on me. The dot-com bubble was blowing up bigger than ever, and we caught the attention of a large VC firm that I will call the Vulture Capitalists. A pure dot-com fund with hundreds of millions invested in everything from medical to music, the Vultures offered us $4 million. That seemed like a staggering amount—by far, our biggest outside investment yet—and would give me a chance to really ride this crazy dot-com wave for all it was worth and let Knit Media grow to its true potential. So I grabbed it.

Now, it appeared, I was really rich. The Vultures got a 20 percent stake, which instantly doubled the company's valuation to a whopping $20 million. That diluted my ownership down to 65 percent, but the higher valuation meant my shares were now worth a bit over $12 million! Once again, I knew that was only on paper. In practical terms, my net worth hadn't budged an inch. Knit Media was only marginally profitable and, every Friday, I still collected a modest paycheck. But, with three outside investors putting in a total of $5 million, we must have been doing something right. "Once we start earning some serious profits," I told myself, "we'll prove that our soaring valuation is well deserved."

How much was Knit Media really worth at that moment? In a sane world, the standard way to calculate the value of a company is using multiples of EBIDTA, a widely used measure of profitability. At ten times our annual EBITDA of $100,000 to $300,000 (depending on the year), Knit Media would be worth $1 million to $3 million—though you might add a bit for the value of the brand name, which had become increasingly familiar to music fans around the world. In the madness of the late '90s, however, using EBITDA to value companies was considered passé and totally inadequate, given the massive potential of the internet.

Then there was the not-so-small matter of what type of shares these Vulture Capitalists were buying. They had demanded Class C *preferred* shares that gave them far more power than the mere *common* shares I owned. My lawyers did a good job of explaining this distinction to me, pointing out that the Vultures really held all the power and riches in this relationship, but their warnings didn't help much. After seeing that piece of paper saying I could be worth $12+ million when, only a few years before, I was sleeping under my desk, well, the hours spent trapped in an office listening to my lawyers drone on about cumulative versus noncumulative preferred stock just made my eyes glaze over. I basically said, "Yeah, yeah, right. Whatever."

The business strategy of my new partners was perfectly in keeping with the dot-com ethos of the time. The Vultures didn't care about building a quality company that would last for generations. They wanted to grow fast and cash out quickly. So they immediately began pushing me to spend their money as fast as humanly possible. It was a land grab, pure and simple, in hopes of instantly becoming a market leader, ranking among the biggest, baddest players in our field.

Along the way, the Vultures didn't care if we, or anybody else in our niche, actually turned a profit. The promise of making a fortune down the road—you know, someday, when this internet thing really takes off—was supposed to inflate the value of Knit Media so high that they could sell their stake at a huge profit to the next starry-eyed investor. It was a high-stakes game of musical chairs because the one left standing when the music stopped would be holding a bag of worthless shares. As long as that sucker wasn't them, the Vultures didn't care. Nothing personal, just business.

So, for the next couple of years, from 1998 to 2000, my job was to grow the company—quickly. "You need to spend money faster, buy more content, develop more content!" the Vultures kept saying. "We need more websites. Hire more programmers!" And spend we did. At our peak, Knit Media had sixty-five web developers, a slew of websites with video, our BET cable TV show, and a record label with hundreds of titles, some obtained by acquiring smaller labels. One of our websites, Jazz-E.com, tried everything to attract clicks, even sponsoring golf tournaments. (I'd make a fortune if I could sell all my leftover Jazz-E.com golf balls and tees!) That's all in addition to our substantial core business of offering Knitting Factory shows and festivals in the US and Europe.

At one point, I was approaching artists like Rashied Ali, the great jazz drummer who played with John Coltrane, and offering him more money than he had ever seen in his life for music rights—not for his studio recordings, but just for internet streaming rights to music sessions he had been holding in his home studio for years. With legal downloading still years away, I wanted to ramp up our businesses of mailing out CDs to customers who ordered them from our website. But the Vultures kept objecting and pushing our streaming services instead, saying, "It's gotta be all digital or it's not worth doing."

Like a lot of internet babble, that made no sense to me. Though I understood the staggering potential of bits and bytes, I also firmly believed in atoms—selling a physical product to generate cash flow and profits. When everybody was predicting the end of "brick and mortar" establishments, I kept insisting there will always be demand for what I called "beer and mortar" companies. "You can't digitize beer," I kept telling the Vultures. And reminding them that people go to nightclubs for more than just music and drinks, I added, "You can't digitize sperm, either."

Clearly, we were not Keeping It Real. Our digital efforts were "pre-revenue," as people used to say, surely one of the most idiotic phrases in business history. It would be easy to make excuses and say nobody kept it real in those days, but that's not quite true. Even Amazon, a risky dot-com if ever there was one—sustaining years of losses—always had, at its core, a transactional model of selling physical objects that people were willing to pay for. For Jeff Bezos, the challenge was hanging in there until enough people connected to the internet and overcame their reluctance to buy things online. He also took the long view, plowing profits back into the company and withstanding Wall Street's skepticism, rather than simply trying to pump up the stock price and then cashing out.

Another entrepreneur who found a way to Keep It Real amid the internet madness is an old friend of mine, Jonathan Nelson. He was an intern at the Knitting Factory back in the early days and helped us build our first website. In 1993, he headed to San Francisco to create Organic, one of the first digital advertising agencies, and took it public just before the dot-com crash in 2000 destroyed its market value. For a minute there, he was my first intern-turned-billionaire. Three years later, Organic was acquired by the Omnicom Group. During his travels, Jonathan learned that the web is just one platform; many others exist in the real world, like billboards and print media, that can be an effective part of a comprehensive media strategy. I'm so proud that Jonathan is now CEO of Omnicom Digital and doing great—and still a good friend—and know that he would not have come this far without finding that delicate balance between analog and digital media.

In retrospect, I should have listened to my gut more. I should have remembered selling broken cookies at the Seven Mile Fair back in Wisconsin and those duffel bags of CDs I sold in Germany, all those great moments that kept business simple, honest, and fun. Instead, I got seduced by the siren song of the Vulture Capitalists. I was like the guy who doesn't fully understand that he's partying with people who are not really his friends, just fellow addicts who will disappear at the first sign of trouble.

By 1999, I was in too deep to back out. Our Digital Club Network continued to grow, bringing in millions in venture capital that summer, though I had so much else going on that I decided to step back to the chairman role and let Andrew run the company as CEO. When Intel left us to partner with a bigger concert company, we didn't break stride, renaming our annual cyber event the Digital Club Festival and booking 300 acts (including Public Enemy and Everlast), whose shows were streamed from twenty clubs in our network. The festival got glowing reviews. "Five years ago, no one took them or what was then known as the Macintosh New York Music Festival too seriously," wrote CNN.com, but now that all the big record labels and concert promoters were jumping on the internet bandwagon, "Rasiej and Dorf had the last laugh."

In my campaign to keep Knit Media tethered to the real world, however precariously, I managed to finally execute a plan I had been dreaming about for years: expanding into a chain of Knitting Factory clubs in sophisticated urban areas across America and around the world—a "Knitwork" of venues, I would call it, all connected by the internet. Eventually, I'd have clubs in ten world capitals, from Berlin to Tokyo to Havana. A music fan in London could be watching, say, a John Zorn show in New York on her laptop when a video-chat box would appear showing someone from Singapore saying, "Wow, what a great show!" Next, someone from Paris might pop up to say, "Oui, he's playing some incredible solos!" I was in love with the idea of creating that kind of exciting digital social interaction around music, the closest thing possible to the actual live experience.

Building a full Knitwork of clubs would take time. I started by opening our second Knitting Factory, this one in Los Angeles. At $4 million, it would not come cheap, and it was certainly not how the Vultures wanted us to spend their money. "We're not in the brick-and-mortar business!" they cried. "We've got to acquire more content!" I explained that we didn't have to *buy* more content because our stages in New York were constantly *generating* huge amounts of content—um, I mean *music*—all streamed and captured by our recording studio. That output would double when we opened in LA, I told them. More importantly, sales of food and drink would produce immediate cash flow and prof-its, however meager, so whatever online sales our shows generated would be a bonus. We could build that part of the business up gradually, over time, as the technology improved.

The Vultures frowned, remaining unconvinced. But I plunged ahead with building what we called the Knitting Factory Hollywood, adding as many technological gimmicks as I could dream up to satisfy both my own urge to experiment and their incessant, internet-centric demands.

By far, my stupidest idea was what I called the "Cones of Silence," named after a device from the old *Get Smart* TV show. To encourage social interaction between people at our two clubs, separated by a continent, a customer in LA could sit at a long table facing a computer screen that showed a video feed of her friend in New York. Hanging about a foot above them would be specially designed plastic cones outfitted with speakers allowing the two people—but no one around them—to hear each other's voices. I wanted to allow private conversations without the hassle of wearing earphones. (The cones would not actually cover people's heads like on *Get Smart*. That would be too stupid, even for me.)

Believe it or not, we actually built the Cones of Silence—at a ridiculously high cost—and installed six each in LA and New York. Nobody used them. Our customers mostly laughed. That's when I should have known things had spiraled out of control. Having the money to spend on something so ludicrous was a sure sign that Knit Media and I were no longer Keeping It Real. The same, of course, could be said for many entrepreneurs who indulged in the excesses of the dot-com era—like the $10 million party in Las Vegas featuring the Who, thrown by Pixelon, a company that would be out of business within a year. But that was faint comfort.

It should have come as no surprise that, on March 11, 2000, the NASDAQ index—which had doubled over the previous year—suddenly began to plunge. As the index lost 10 percent of its value in a matter of weeks, the tech world's worst fear was coming true: We were all partying inside a tech bubble that was bursting, spectacularly. By the end of the following year, trillions of dollars in investment capital would simply disappear.

My Vulture Capitalist partners started to panic. This was not the outcome they envisioned at all. The music had stopped, the record industry was broken, and now they were left holding a bunch of Knit Media shares worth a fraction of their former value. They decided to bail out immediately.

The lead investor called me to break the news: They were liquidating their fund and sending all their dot-coms into bankruptcy—including us.

"But we're not really a dot-com!" I cried. "We have a profitable club in New York and now a new one coming in LA—"

"I don't give a shit," he said. "I don't know if you read those legal documents you signed, but we control the company now. And we're closing you down."

This was bad. I had to decide what to do—fast. I was like, "The fuck you are."

4

To Thine Own Wine Be True

With apologies to the Bard, in this chapter title, I'm tinkering with the wise counsel of Polonius in *Hamlet* to make a point: After the dot-com bust, taking refuge in the rich, sensory world of wine-making and listening to live jazz helped me discover a new purpose in life. That kind of self-knowledge, I'm convinced, is essential to being successful in business.

After all, how can you satisfy the needs and desires of customers if you don't understand those needs yourself in a visceral, personal way? When so much of the business world is rushing into a blind embrace of all things digital, I'm inspired by entrepreneurs who ignore the outside chatter and focus instead on the inner voice that leads them to some unmet need.

Take the Italian designer Maria Sebregondi. She was irked at being unable to buy the type of simple oilcloth notebooks that Matisse, Picasso, and Hemingway once used. That led her to introduce Moleskine, which became a runaway success, treasured by a worldwide community of writers, artists, and creative professionals. The need she identified was simple. "Our ideas are more tangible and real when we can see them physically," she said.

How about SoulCycle founders Ruth Zukerman, Elizabeth Cutler, and Julie Rice, who grew tired of fitness routines that felt too much like work? Rather than trying to jazz things up with digital distractions, as so many in the fitness world were doing, they harnessed the power of physical community to create something new: joyful and inspiring stationary-bike workouts. SoulCycle became a cultural phenomenon and is now owned by one of the largest real estate developers in the United States, with nearly ninety studios throughout North America.

Richard Branson, a hero of mine, started both Virgin Records and Virgin Atlantic to satisfy his own needs when it came to music and air travel. He sums up the lesson well: "There is no point in starting your own business unless you do it out of a sense of frustration."

Amen. For me, the frustration occurred when I reached my late thirties and early forties and could not find a nightclub in New York City where I could sit down comfortably, enjoy a great meal and glass of wine, and see the bands I loved. That's what led me to start City Winery. But I'm getting ahead of myself. All that would come later. First, I had to survive a showdown with my Vulture Capitalist partners who were hell-bent on destroying my company—and, by extension, me.

For months after the dot-com party ended in the spring of 2000, I was stumbling around, half-crocked on internet moonshine, trying to get my bearings.

In truth, things had started falling apart well before that. Our new Knitting Factory in Los Angeles, which was supposed to be an island of stability amid all the tech craziness, was in deep trouble. Delays and cost overruns had gotten so out of hand that the contractor demanded that I come up with $1.8 million or he would walk off the job.

I was shocked. Our new club on Hollywood Boulevard was supposed to be my crowning achievement–a 10,000-square-foot entertainment complex with a large performance area for 300 to 400 music fans; a smaller, intimate venue for more adventurous programming seating forty to fifty people; and a separate restaurant-bar area. I wanted to book a mix of what I called the "blue-chip avant-garde" (Laurie Anderson, Lou Reed, Philip Glass); the best contemporary jazz musicians (Leon Parker, Henry Threadgill, Ravi Coltrane); and artist/tastemakers such as They Might Be Giants and the Violent Femmes, who had already played the East Coast Knit. Eventually, our LA club could become a springboard to creating a major jazz festival similar to what I had been producing in New York.

Now the whole enterprise was about to go up in smoke if I didn't submit to the demands of a sleazy contractor who had me by the balls. We had nowhere near that kind of cash lying around.

Knit Media did, however, own a 20 percent share in the Digital Club Network. Despite the faltering dot-com market, DCN was going strong, attracting venture capitalists with our pitch that archival footage of obscure bands would someday become immensely valuable once those artists made it big. (Imagine recording the Beatles live in Liverpool before anyone had ever heard of them, then multiply that by hundreds; near-term revenue would come from advertising and sponsorships of webcasts from our global network of nightclubs.) I still had high hopes for this business model, even if it was ahead of its time, but now I was desperate.

Frantically, I sent a group email to all eight members of the Knit Media board asking for approval of the sale of our stake: "I really think DCN is overvalued," I wrote. "The hype has gotten totally out of control and the chances of DCN ever making much money in the short-term is next to zero. So I think we should sell our DCN stock immediately and put it into finishing the LA club, which will soon be generating a strong monthly cash flow."

A reasonable argument, I thought. But when I got a quick reply from my partner, DCN chief executive Andrew Rasiej—"WTF??!!!"—I froze in horror. Oh, shit: I had accidentally sent it to the wrong board, a *different* group of eight recipients—the DCN board!

This was awful. Trashing DCN to its own board, which included the one member who might be willing to buy out our shares? After some screaming and tearing my hair out—what was left of it, anyway—I quickly wrote another note explaining that, ahem, the previous email was actually meant for the Knit Media board. "I really don't feel that way," I wrote. "In fact, I feel just the opposite. But there are some real internet believers on the Knit board who love DCN, so I had to badmouth the whole concept to convince them to sell."

Thanks to some extremely understanding DCN board members, the sale was ultimately approved for about $2 million. Thankfully, I was able to pay off the sleazy contractor to finish the LA club, and learned some huge lessons along the way: 1) Vet your contractors closely. 2) Be extremely careful before hitting "send"!

My proceeds from that rushed sale were far less than the paper value of our DCN stake at the time—VCs were valuing the company at $50 million, making our share worth, in theory, about $10 million. In retrospect, however, it was a smart move: DCN soon went bust as the dot-com sector continued to implode. As Andrew said later, mostly in jest, "Michael Dorf (the fu*#ker) was the only one who made money!" Turns out DCN's investors were not patient enough to wait for years until artists like John Legend, whom we recorded in a small New York club early in his career, became famous. And more immediate revenue from streaming live shows never materialized. That's partly because video quality was so poor in those low-bandwidth days, but also because live concerts, aside from the occasional pay-per-view program, are simply not compelling enough to watch on a screen. Even a slick production, the market seemed to be saying, can't replicate the experience of hanging out with friends watching a live show by a great band—something I gradually came to understand myself.

No sooner had that crisis been averted than the Vulture Capitalists informed me that my life's work was about to evaporate in a flash. With the dot-com market tanking, they were liquidating their entire fund for pennies on the dollar. They told me they would be dumping their entire $4 million stake in Knit Media for a quarter of what they paid for it—by writing it off or selling to the first buyer offering $1 million. If they didn't find a buyer, they would file for Chapter 7 bankruptcy. As they never seemed to tire of reminding me, even though they owned only 20 percent of the company, all those blasted special preferred shares gave them the power to do whatever the hell they wanted. (Note to self: Listen carefully to your friggin' lawyers!)

Once again, I went into panic mode. "Give me a few weeks," I begged the Vultures, "and I'll come up with $1 million in cash."

Working my contacts madly, I was connected to a wealthy New York investor with a passion for music. When I traveled to his home in a rich suburb, he took me into his spacious bedroom, where he had stacks and stacks of vinyl records piled high. Clearly, this guy was no mere hobbyist—he was a serious fan and student of all kinds of music. We talked for a long time. He said he loved what we were doing, appreciated the musical integrity of our artists, and agreed to buy out the Vulture Capitalists for $1 million. I breathed a sigh of relief. The Wealthy Patron had saved the day—at least for now.

The devil, of course, is in the details, as the Vultures had taught me. I was still in the middle of negotiating the deal when Sarah and I got on a plane in May of 2000 for what was supposed to be the greatest honor of my life: I had been chosen to give the commencement speech at our alma mater, Washington University in St. Louis.

I was going to be celebrated for my business achievements, and a group of dear friends were flying in for the occasion. But when I arrived on campus, I could not relax and enjoy it. I had to skip the chancellor's reception and the dean's dinner because I was holed up in my hotel, faxing documents back and forth with my new investor, knowing that the fate of the company I had spent fourteen years nurturing hung in the balance. I sent Sarah and my friends, all bemused by the irony and teasing me mercilessly, to say that I was not feeling well and was unable to leave the hotel until the speech.

When I stepped onto the stage for the graduation ceremony, I really did feel sick—a combination of nerves, facing thousands of people, and my desperate need to close the deal back in New York. After being introduced as founder of the world-famous Knitting Factory, "one of the ten most influential New Yorkers," and "a leader in the convergence of music and technology," I shakily approached the podium.

"Sixteen short years ago, I was sitting in the quad listening to Bob Hope talking about the future as I was graduating from Wash U," I began, but I felt like a bigger joker than Bob Hope. As I rambled on about our "newly wired world moving at exponential speeds with new paradigms for doing business" and dropped names like Lou Reed, Laurie Anderson, and Pat Metheny, I couldn't stop thinking, *What a fraud! If they only knew.*

When the ceremony was over, I rushed back to the hotel and more faxes. To add insult to injury, the hotel kept running out of fax paper, driving my stress levels even higher. (Be thankful for your smartphones, kids.) Man, it was hell.

At last, the deal was done, though I'm embarrassed to admit I did not fully understand that the terms of this contract were more challenging than my deal with the Vultures. The Wealthy Patron ended up investing a total of $2 million—$1 million to buy out the Vultures and the rest for operating expenses–but he had shrewdly structured the deal as a convertible loan that allowed him to gain more shares in the company as interest payments. He could also convert the loan's principle to an ownership stake anytime he wanted–and, since the funds were coming in as debt, his stake was senior to all other investments or stock in the company. He certainly was smarter than me. Being desperate, I took the deal.

The upshot was that, once again, I had no control over my own damn company. I was frustrated, and later wondered how I could have let it happen.

Looking back, I realized that one mistake I made was taking the wrong way some great advice my father had given me. A few years earlier, when I had the chance to bring in my first outside investor, I didn't know what to do. The whole idea of diluting my ownership was foreign to me, and a little scary. It was also foreign to my Dad, who, along with my uncle and grandfather always had 100 percent family ownership of the Milwaukee Biscuit Company. My grandfather Sol never considered the concept of outside investors. He founded the company to be built to last, to pass down to his family. But, in discussing it with my Dad, he said something I have never forgotten: "It's better to own 5 percent of gold than 100 percent of shit." By that, of course, he meant that it's much better to own a smaller percentage of a top-notch, high-valuation company than to own a high percentage of a crappy underperformer. Hard to argue with that, right? My first investors were high-integrity pros with great ideas about growing the company by stressing business fundamentals and they were in it for the long haul. Bringing them on with a $500,000 investment for 10 percent of the company was a no-brainer.

The problem, of course, came when I brought in those Vulture Capitalists two years later. Their short-sighted greed helped turn my piece of gold to shit–though I knew I was ultimately responsible for what happened. Even after I brought in the Wealthy Patron in 2000, I retained the titles of chairman and chief executive of Knit Media but had an extremely weak position that gave me little stock value or ultimate decision making.

At least the company was still functioning, I told myself. Being an optimist who's been in plenty of dire situations before, I saw bright days ahead of us, especially once this little dot-com stock-market correction settled down and things we had been predicting for years–legal downloads and streaming music–finally came to fruition. Our vast catalog of music under the Knit brand would only become more valuable as these new distribution channels matured. Besides, I was far too busy to pout. Bell Atlantic had re-upped as sponsor of our jazz festival, this time for a whopping $2 million. That made the June 2000 event our biggest by far–250 concerts in four cities (New York, Boston, Philadelphia, and Washington, D.C.) with headliners like Chick Corea, Los Lobos, and Ornette Coleman.

Most satisfying was seeing our LA Knitting Factory, after endless delays, finally opening in August. In our hallway, we had a line of eight interactive kiosks, each sponsored by a music tech company for $25,000 (not knowing that all eight firms would be out of business or sold within a year). We also rolled out my futuristic Cones of Silence that I was sure would transform the social lives of customers on both coasts. Oh, and there was live music too—with opening night featuring the Seattle alt-pop band the Posies along with local groups like Whiskey Biscuit and Beachwood Sparks.

All my optimism and hard work could not stop Knit Media's downward spiral, however. With investment sources drying up, our Internet operations still hemorrhaging red ink, our LA club losing money, and New York only barely profitable, I had no choice but to drastically downsize the company. That meant massive layoffs. It was a painful experience for everyone. I had to let go scores of web developers, graphic designers, accounting staff, record-label employees, and more. It was especially tough to have to shut down the whole video-production department, which meant my talented friend Mitch Goldman and his TV team, who had done such great work capturing our live shows and producing *Live from the Knitting Factory*.

By the summer of 2001, I looked washed up. With the economy now in recession, our jazz festival sponsorships disappeared, and, for the first time in fourteen years, we did not put on a big summer event. In an article about my troubles, *The New York Times* quoted George Wein as saying, "I wouldn't bet, financially, on his future at the moment." (Though I was encouraged to see him add, "But I would bet on his future 10 years from now.")

In other words, the pounding hangover from my high-tech partying had officially begun. But I hadn't hit bottom yet. That would not happen until one morning in September of 2001, as I was running on a treadmill at a gym on Leonard Street, next to the Knitting Factory.

It was a beautiful, sunny day, the sky a deep blue. Through the windows of the gym, I saw a commotion outside. I hopped off the machine, walked out to the corner of Leonard and Church Streets, and looked up to see smoke pouring from the World Trade Center, about twelve blocks away.

My mind raced. That morning, Sarah and I had both left our apartment early—she went uptown to work on a film—and our nanny Shamiza had said she might bring our three-year-old twins to the World Trade Center, since we lived nearby. There was a Barnes & Noble inside the complex, and Eli and Zachary loved hanging out in the kids' section, playing and looking at picture books.

I called Shamiza immediately. Thankfully, she picked up. "There was an accident at the World Trade Center," I told her, "so, if you hurry, you can bring the boys down there to see the fire trucks. You know how much they love fire trucks."

Satisfied that I had performed my fatherly duties, I went back into the club and resumed my workout. Just another day of calamity in Manhattan—one day, it's a busted water main, the next it's ambulances racing to a fire. Then, a few minutes later, I watched CNN on the gym TVs reporting that an airplane had hit Tower 1 and showing live footage of a second plane hitting Tower 2. I rushed out to the street again. Oh, my God! I called Shamiza back. It seemed like forever before she finally answered. They had not left yet. Thank God. "Stay home," I said. "Don't go anywhere."

On the street, people were freaking out—running up Church Street, away from the smoking towers. I recognized a friend I had hired for productions, who looked completely dazed. He had been getting a stage ready for a dance concert in the plaza between the two towers, he said, and hid underneath the stage when he heard the sirens. Then he heard some loud thumps above him. When he emerged, he realized the sound had come from bodies dropping onto the stage. He was in such shock that I spent a few minutes trying to console him.

I knew I had to get home quickly, collect my family, and get the hell out of there. Clearly, we were under attack; people were saying the Pentagon had also been hit. I called Sarah at her midtown studio and we decided to drive to our home upstate. If the cell-phone towers go down, we would meet at the on-ramp to the George Washington bridge. Then I ran to the office, sent the accounting team home (the only early birds at the office), and stuffed my backpack with incorporation papers, insurance documents, anything that seemed important.

I ran toward my car. After about a block, I turned around and hustled back, realizing that I was not bringing survival priorities. Who needs paperwork? It's the end of the world! I grabbed cash from our safe, twenty-four bottles of water, and two bottles of Macallan scotch. (Somehow, the scotch seemed important.) Lugging that heavy load, I ran west across Leonard, crossing avenues filled with people running north, and got my car from the lot next to the Tribeca Grill. There was no time to obey traffic laws, so I drove the wrong way up Greenwich Street a few blocks to our apartment, dodging fire trucks, armored police vehicles, and tanks—yes, blue NYPD tanks! *Where the hell do they house those?* I wondered—all of them racing toward the battle zone.

When I got home, Shamiza and the boys were safe. At their age, the twins had no idea what was going on. Sarah made it home later, after walking most of the way from midtown, but our escape plan was scuttled. The streets below Canal, including ours, had been closed to all but emergency vehicles.

With everyone safe in our apartment by 11:15 a.m. or so, I went outside to survey the scene and check up on some new friends I had made at Tribeca Wine Merchants. That's when I watched Tower 1 crumbling to dust, as if in slow motion. The horrific image remains seared in my memory, impossible to forget.

After two nights, we were finally able to drive upstate to escape the stench and breathe some fresh country air. About a week later, we returned to a neighborhood that looked like a war zone, complete with military checkpoints. Only people who could prove residency were allowed in. With no customers at the Knitting Factory, I decided to open the doors for emergency workers. For the next six weeks, we distributed free food, beer, and water to police, firefighters, and volunteers who needed a place to rest and recover from their grueling work.

It was the least we could do—and I was glad to help our community. Financially, however, it was devastating. Our New York club, Knit Media's only reliable source of revenue, had no income for nearly two months. Our LA club also took a big hit when the tourism industry declined substantially after 9/11 and the national economy slid deeper into recession.

That was probably my lowest point. As if the dot-com bust, destruction of the record business, and a national recession weren't bad enough, now a terrorist attack had destroyed our neighborhood. Scrambling again, I was forced to borrow more money from the Wealthy Patron, putting the company further in debt and giving his faction on the board even more control. At least they were keeping us on life support.

Now I was in a funk. The destruction I'd witnessed was immense, and thousands had died—though, thankfully, no one I knew. For the first time in my life, I wasn't enjoying my work. I really don't think it was 9/11-induced depression. I just wanted to get back to work and start rebuilding the company, but the company's balance sheet, full of red ink, made that impossible. We were in survival mode. And, with all the convertible debt and those friggin' preferred shares, I was not the boss anymore.

That was a real problem. I'd never *had* a boss before. Hell, I'd never had a *job* before, or a résumé. I've always been a self-made man, an entrepreneur with complete freedom to follow my whims, wherever they might lead. Now that I had a boss, the board and I clashed constantly about everything, from big issues to small ones.

One of our worst fights was about opening a Knitting Factory in Paris. This was an idea I'd had for a long time and become serious about when three guys who ran a French record company—and distributed some of our titles there—wanted to become partners in the venture. They were convinced our club concept could do well in Paris, which has always been enthusiastic about American jazz and our brand, in particular. We found a space in the hip 11th arrondissement, created a business plan, and lined up about $2 million in local financing. I was excited and loved spending so much time in that beautiful city.

When I presented the contracts to the Knit Media board members, they noticed a clause that said I would oversee the building and running of the new club for the next three years, regardless of my position in the company. "We can't believe you'd put this in for your own protection!" one board member snapped.

"That's not what happened," I protested. My French partners, who had sensed that things were not going smoothly back in New York, had inserted this "key-man" language to make sure that I was in charge of the project, not someone they didn't know. In fact, they insisted upon it. To them, I *was* the Knitting Factory.

The Wealthy Patron and his sympathetic board members didn't believe me. They considered it a sneaky power grab. "That's it," he said. "The deal is over." This wonderful idea—the Knitting Factory Paris—never materialized.

Another deflating moment came when a guy I'd hired to run our record label made a decision that infuriated me. He was a smart operator who built a successful label that we had bought during our spending spree. With money tight, he urged us to focus on only a few of our biggest-selling titles and abandon the rest. I disagreed, but his next step was even worse. To save storage space, he wanted to destroy all those unwanted CDs in our inventory—more than 100,000 units.

Such an extreme measure might make sense for a major label, but not for an independent like us. We could have sold them for twenty dollars apiece by internet mail order to music lovers all over the world. If we were really just cleaning out the basement, why not sell them cheaply to the artists them-selves, who could sell them on their tours? Hell, we could have *given* them away to the musicians as a bonus. That would create amazing goodwill, and we'd get our basement cleaned for free. The board hated my idea, mostly because it came from me, since they were opposing everything I suggested. One morning, I came in to witness a terrible sight: Two dump trucks and about eight workers throwing thousands of CDs away. So senseless. All that great music, lost.

By then, I was truly distraught. Was this how I wanted to spend my life, fighting over idiotic stuff like this? Watching all my ideas get shot down? At this point, I was doing little more than selling drinks to support my family. Where's the joy in that? I had just turned forty years old, was going bald, and had two kids. Between those milestones and 9/11, I was thinking a lot about how precious and fleeting life is. This was no way to live.

Deep down, I knew it was time to leave the Knit. The board clearly wanted me out. They didn't have the nerve to fire me and were obviously hoping I'd leave voluntarily. After much anguish, I finally decided to resign as CEO–letting them run things the way they want–but stay on as chairman of the board. After all, the Knitting Factory was my baby. How could I let it go completely?

That created a new problem: Now what would I do with myself? I had no answers, only questions. And those are the uncomfortable moments, I've noticed, when the most inter-esting part of a person's life begins.

In late 2002, I got a phone call that helped me real-ize what I'd really like to do next. It was from the Lower

Manhattan Development Corporation, which was leading the reconstruction of Ground Zero. Anita Contini, director of memorial and cultural programs, said there was tremendous interest in—and a great deal of funding for—a major performance center at the site. They had conducted surveys showing that two of the top five cultural memories people had of the World Trade Center were concerts I had produced—including a day of New Orleans music featuring the Neville Brothers and The Meters. (I remembered that one well—a truly magical day of music.) Could I put together a proposal of my vision for a new arts center?

What an opportunity! I already had an idea, something I had been thinking about for a while. By then, I had started going out to hear music again, realizing how much I missed it, and became annoyed that so many nightclubs were geared only toward the younger generation. They were ignoring customers like me: people aged forty-plus who don't want to stand on sticky floors holding a plastic beer cup anymore. Where were the comfortable rooms that let you sit down and enjoy great food and wine while catching a show by Jeff Tweedy or Suzanne Vega? A place more relaxed and mature than the Knit was when I founded it fifteen years earlier.

When Anita called, I saw my chance to not only develop this concept, but also help revive my struggling neighborhood. I called it the World Arts Center with the tagline: "A downtown Carnegie Hall with a great wine list."

That was a turning point. Working on such an exciting idea made me realize how uninspired I truly was at the Knit under its new leadership. It was the motivation I needed to finally say, once and for all, "Fuck it. Fuck the new investors. I'm moving on." At the end of 2003, after frustrating negotiations and litigation, I decided to cut the cord completely—resigned as chairman, sold my shares, and no longer had any connection to the company.

It took a while to extract the proceeds from that sale, which ended up totaling about $150,000. (I got two extra provisions in my exit agreement that seemed critical at the time: 1) They couldn't erase me from the history of the club online; and 2) I could get free drinks and admission whenever I wanted.) That's a far cry from the $12 million I thought I was worth back when the company had a sky-high valuation just a few years earlier, but I felt lucky to walk away with anything at all. Though I saw the folly of some of my decisions, I never regretted a moment of that wild ride. And, while I was bitter at the new investors, I was also grateful that they had kept Knit Media alive, still believing in its long-term viability. In time, the Los Angeles Knit would lose its luster and close. The Manhattan venue moved to a smaller space in Brooklyn. But, over the years, the brand actually extended its reach as the company, now called Knitting Factory Entertainment, acquired clubs around the country, in places like Boise, Idaho, and Spokane, Washington, and renamed them the Knitting Factory.

As time went on, I became proud of the fact that the brand I spent so much of my life developing was still powerful enough to attract music fans. This hit home during one of the mountain trips I take every year with some old pals. One night, we ended up in Boise after seven days of hiking and climbing in Utah. As we drove to the hotel, dirty and smelly from the trip, my friend Pete Ostrow noticed a sign for the local Knitting Factory. He kept ribbing me, "Hey, let's go there tonight, see if they know you. We'll get those free drinks they promised you!" Since leaving the Knit, I had never gone back to claim my drinks or see a show—I guess I still hadn't resolved my complicated feelings about the place. I figured, "What the hell" and contacted the venue. They didn't know who I was, so I emailed the CEO, who alerted the club. A few hours later, showered and clean, we walked into the club and they rolled out the red carpet for us. The ear-splitting metal music was not our thing, so we left after one drink. But for one night at least, in the middle of Idaho, it was humbling to be recognized as the founder of a brand that still stands for something—qualities like musical adventurousness, integrity, and hipness. That feels like a legacy.

Back in 2003, after taking my exit package, there was some sadness about leaving the Knit. But I was too excited about my new idea to wallow for long (and I'm not really the wallowing type). When the endless debates and hyper-emotional controversies over rebuilding the World Trade Center dragged on and my proposal for a World Arts Center languished, I didn't give up, coming up with a new idea to renovate an old bank on Wall Street for a nightspot called The Art Exchange. I used the same tagline: "A downtown Carnegie Hall with a great wine list!" and sent around a business plan that estimated it would cost $20 million to launch. Alas, I couldn't find a single investor willing to say, "A big, expensive concert facility on Wall Street? Hey, great idea!"

By 2004, I was unemployed with no viable prospects. Sarah and I had had our third child, Sophia, the previous December. With three kids to support, it was a scary time.

We stayed afloat thanks to Sarah's movie-producing work and by refinancing our Tribeca apartment, which continued to appreciate despite the 9/11 tragedy.

To keep myself busy, I teamed up with five other families to create an after-school program called Tribeca Hebrew to help our children and others in our neighborhood develop their Jewish identities. There was a big demand for it. The community just needed some schmuck like me to say, "Hey, let's just rent this tiny storefront and fix it up!" Within three years, it grew to more than 120 kids. We merged it with another local Jewish learning center and, today, it's still going strong.

I also started a series of tribute concerts at Carnegie Hall to raise money for music education. Again, I received some sage advice from my father, who said to make sure I associated my name with it by calling it "Michael Dorf Presents." I should go on stage and make the introductions, he said—start thinking of myself as part of the brand. I did, and, after fifteen years, I'm proud to say, "The Music of..." series has become something of an institution. Each year, we gather an amazing group of artists to interpret the music of a legendary figure. We started with Joni Mitchell the first year, followed by Bob Dylan, then Bruce Springsteen, all the way to our most recent tribute to Van Morrison in 2019.

Carnegie Hall is not cheap, so neither are the tickets, but we sell out every year, thanks to an all-star cast of musicians that, over the years, has included Patti Smith, Bobby McFerrin, Neil Sedaka, Aaron Neville, the Roots, and so many others. I'm amazed and humbled at how, for a minimal honorarium, all the artists work so hard to create unique cover versions of songs by the legends who inspired them. Sometimes, the legend being celebrated actually shows up, as was the case with Springsteen, Michael Stipe, and David Byrne (who brought a marching band down the aisle for the encore). Before the first event, Joni Mitchell called me at the last minute to say she could not come because her beloved cat got sick, but she sent sixty yellow long-stemmed roses, one for each musician, each with a thank-you note. That quickly became a tradition: I began giving each musician a yellow rose as they come off the stage. Best of all, it's been thrilling to raise a total of $1.6 million (so far) for music programs for underserved kids.

It was during this time, while experiencing the joy of giving back–and shamelessly promoting myself as the organizer of the Carnegie Hall tribute concerts–that I began drifting toward the field that would finally give me the precise direction I needed: making wine.

I had always been an avid consumer of wine, starting in college when I brought home a bottle of Beaujolais Nouveau. Our family was never a group of wine drinkers and my Uncle Shelly teasingly called me "Mr. Beaujolais." Then there were those pretentious Technology & Wine dinners I threw for my upscale digerati friends during the dot-com years. And I'll never forget an incredibly romantic trip to Montrachet, France, with Sarah to sample the region's amazing vintages in the early '90s, shortly after we married.

It was not until I got a call from my brother Josh that I ever imagined I could fall in love with the elaborate process of *producing* wine. The great winemaker David Tate, whom Josh knew well, was sitting on 2,500 pounds of fabulous

Cabernet that his winery in Cupertino, California, didn't need. Maybe I'd like to spend a few thousand dollars to join Josh in buying up the grapes and making our own barrels of wine? That sounded like fun and a great chance to spend time with my brother. Despite his being seven years younger than me, Josh and I have always been close. He helped build the Knitting Factory's first website, staffed our Amsterdam office, and has been a crucial adviser and confidant over the years. Josh really knows his stuff: After working at a variety of Bay Area dot-com startups over the years, including the website that became wine.com, he's now the CEO of the Stone Buhr Flour Company, a natural-food brand popular in the Northwest.

Making that wine with Josh was an incredible, eye-opening experience. (We were also joined by our friend, Jonathan Nelson, the intern-turned-billionaire, and my mountain-climbing buddy Pete Ostrow.) After going through the entire vinification process—crushing the grapes, watching them ferment, tinkering with the taste—I could see what a joyful challenge this was. On one hand, you have to think like an engineer and understand the chemistry and physics involved. But it's also an art, requiring that you improvise like a jazz musician or a painter: After being deeply schooled in technique, you can let loose and create, making on-the-fly decisions based on your intuition. Sort of like—no, make that *exactly* like—being an entrepreneur.

We had a blast. Sixteen months later, we found ourselves happily hand-corking 700 bottles with labels custom-made by another friend, the painter Dan Bodner. Dan used a beautiful painting he did of a little shed on a ridge. How cool this custom-wine project was!

Later, I came to understand why this experience grabbed me so strongly: My hangover from the dot-com party of the '90s had made me crave something real, something I could touch and feel, unlike the digital world with its seductive illusions. If Nicholas Negroponte got me excited about the weightless world of computerized bits, wine-making pulled me back to the physical universe of atoms. In those grapes, in the dirt and vines from which they emerged, and, with all the capriciousness of (and dependency upon) mother nature, the *terroir*, in French wine-speak, I finally felt grounded again.

Together with the live music I was hearing at authentic and gritty places like the Village Vanguard—a fantastic listening room—wine-making helped me appreciate the sensory world in a way I never had before. I saw the complexity of the world, its deeper meaning—like Candide realizing that even the plunder of kings cannot compare with the garden he returns to at the end of the story.

In all my scuffling around, I was coming to understand my own needs and desires: live music, a comfortable place to enjoy it, and making wine. I just didn't have a clue about how to make a viable business out of it.

5

Taste the Music, Hear the Food, See the Wine

This nonsensical riff comes from City Winery's marketing materials that play around with our mantra, "Indulge Your Senses." But behind the fun lies a strong conviction of mine: Companies that can appeal to the visceral, sensory aspects of our lives today are gaining a crucial competitive edge.

Don't take my word for it. Just look around at the scores of firms thriving by selling *experiences*, sometimes one stacked on top of the other to generate the biggest rush: sports centers like Topgolf that allow you to tee up on a driving range while you enjoy food, drink, and music with your friends; "paint 'n' sip" art studios where you can imbibe while unleashing your inner Rembrandt; comfortable movie theaters offering a full menu of entrees and craft beers; once-corny bowling alleys and ice-skating rinks transformed into trendy and flirtatious nights out; Punch Bowl Social, with its multisensory activities from bocce to karaoke surrounded by great food and beverage; indoor skydiving companies like I-fly that let you magically float on a cushion of air roaring up through a tall plexiglass column; and football, basketball, and baseball games that have become as much a culinary experience as a sporting event. The list goes on.

I'm exposed to this trend frequently because commercial real-estate agents—saddled with acres of empty stores as Amazon steals foot traffic—often call me after hearing that we offer an *"experiential"* product. That's their favorite buzzword these days, one I noticed Howard Schultz used when he announced that Starbucks was closing its online store to focus on improving its physical locations. "Every retailer that is going to win in this new environment must become an experiential destination," he told investors shortly before stepping down as CEO. "Your product and services, for the most part, cannot be available online and cannot be available on Amazon."

Even Amazon knows that the Death of Retail has been greatly exaggerated because the vast majority of retail revenue still comes from physical stores. That's why Jeff Bezos has been buying and opening so many of them in recent years. He understands, as Steve Jobs did, that in many cases, people still want to touch and feel the merchandise.

Yet stores can't survive today selling products alone. They need to give customers a good reason to spend their precious time on a visit. That's why you'll find yourself being offered a facial and makeup lesson at Sephora. And why Matches Fashion, once a brick-and-mortar store that now rings up 95 percent of its sales online, stages an "In Residence" series offering talks, meetings with fashion designers, movie showings, exercise classes, and lessons in floristry and social media.

"You need to be accessible to your customer wherever she wants to find you," the company's CEO Tom Chapman has said, "and we have seen that a sizable proportion want human interaction."

In my business, providing a compelling sensory experience was never the problem. If I know anything, it's how to put on a show. But, in the aughts, as the invention of the iPhone and Facebook accelerated our shift toward virtual experiences, my biggest challenge was figuring out how to make a living for everybody—from the musicians to the service staff to investors, and, of course, yours truly—by presenting the real thing.

The answer, I was surprised to discover, was right in front of me the whole time, swishing around in the belly of my wine glass.

When I discovered wine-making, I was surprised to learn that what emerges from the barrel is a living, almost breathing thing. From the first taste of grapes on the vine to sipping the wine as it ferments, then sampling it in the barrel—and again at three months, at six months, and beyond—the wine is constantly evolving. It reminded me of the development of my twin boys. Zachary, our firstborn by a minute, was pushing Eli around in the womb until the moment he took his first breath. Even today, Zach likes being the first out the door, the first to sit at the table for dinner. You might say his personality was set before he was uncorked.

The same thing happens with wine. You can taste the nuances of the grape through the entire process. Like a child,

the wine matures, develops, and grows ever more complex–
but you can still taste the very same elements back when the
grapes were still on the vine. You could say the womb is the
terroir, a metaphysical concept that includes conditions like
altitude and all of nature's elements: the amount of ultravi-
olet light, the wind, the temperature, and, of course, more
than anything, the soil. *Terroir* is that unique place on the
planet best suited for a particular type of grape.

I remember during my trip to Montrachet in France
with Sarah, we saw a grower who seemed to be stroking
his vines and gently singing to them as he pruned. It was a
beautiful, intimate moment that showed how much he cared
about those old and valuable vines. Moments like that moved
me and deepened my curiosity. The more I learned about
wine-making, the more I realized how simple the basics
are: When grapes are crushed, the natural yeast on the skin
comes into contact with the sugars inside, turning them
into alcohol. From that moment on, the winemaker needs to
focus on keeping the process as clean and natural as possible. The best wine is produced with minimal intervention,
just respect and the wisdom and instinct to know when to
put the wine into what kind of barrel, and when to remove
it and put it into a bottle. The wine continues to evolve until
the day–maybe a year, maybe thirty years–when it's perfect
to drink. That is so fucking cool.

No classes or wine dinners ever gave me that level of
insight. It was the wine-making experience, the hands-on
participation in the process, that really hooked me. I needed
to make wine every year. When I gave my friends a bottle
with my name on the label, and talked about the adventure of

making it, they said, "Hey, I wanna do that too!" That's when I realized that helping people make their own wine could be a great business, and a fantastic way to spend my days.

What such a business would look like remained vague until the summer of 2005, when I took my family to Oregon's Willamette Valley. It was supposed to be a family vacation—Zachary and Eli were nearly seven and Sophia about 18 months—but I had an ulterior motive: I wanted to visit a bunch of my favorite wineries, including two exceptional ones, Domaine Drouhin and Archery Summit, located in one of my favorite spots, the Dundee Hills.

I had been turned on to Domaine Drouhin nearly a decade earlier by Timothy Greenfield-Sanders, the photographer and filmmaker who was working on a documentary about Lou Reed. One night, Lou brought him backstage at the Knitting Factory. Timothy had brought a bottle of the winery's 1994 Pinot Noir and it only took a few sips for Lou and me to both fall in love with it. A couple of years later, Lou and Laurie Anderson invited Sarah and me to dinner at their new apartment in the West Village. I was so excited that I hunted all over the place until I finally tracked down a magnum of the exact same vintage. When we arrived, Lou began showing me his office/studio and I proudly presented him with my gift. He grinned, gave me a bear hug, and, from a drawer in his desk, pulled out a magnum of the very same 1994 Domaine Drouhin Pinot Noir he had found for our dinner. We had a good laugh over that.

Immediately, we started enjoying the wine, but over the course of the evening, I drank twice as much as Lou and Laurie because I was sipping constantly from Sarah's glass.

We had just learned that she was pregnant with the twins and didn't want anyone to know yet. I got so sloshed that I lost all inhibitions and stopped trying to be cool around Lou. I started gushing like a teenage fanboy about how I couldn't believe I was sitting with Lou Reed, told him how much I adored the Velvet Underground, and barraged him with questions about the band, hanging out with Andy Warhol and playing with David Bowie. It was my big chance to vicariously experience Lou's amazing life. The cosmic joke is that I got so drunk I can't remember a thing he told me!

Anyway, back to our wine trip to Oregon. Sarah and I had dragged the kids to a tasting at Domaine Drouhin, and on the drive back to our bed and breakfast, the family was asleep—the kids in the back and Sarah in the passenger seat. Still a little elated from the last tasting stop, I saw a "For Sale" sign at the top of a hill and stopped the car. I got out, walked around the property and called the number on the sign. Someone answered and said the price was $2 million something. Hmmm, interesting. That was about the value of our Tribeca apartment and everything in it.

I got back into the car, woke everyone up, and called a family meeting. I told them that, like Voltaire, I wanted to get back to the garden. And I needed a career change, so why not open a winery? Wouldn't this be a fantastic place to live? I was dead serious. The boys, bored out of their minds already during our tasting tour, screamed in unison, "No fucking way, Dad!" Sophia babbled that she agreed with her brothers. Sarah, who normally would be mad at the boys for swearing, fully supported their profane statement and even noted that they had used the right intonation.

At that moment, I realized that, if I wanted to make wine and keep my family, I would have to do it in New York City. That sounded ridiculous at first—a winery in the middle of Manhattan?—but, the more I thought about it, the less far-fetched it seemed. My mind started spinning: In the culture at large for a long time, and especially in progressive urban areas, there had been a huge interest in where our food originates. Inspired by writers like Michael Pollan and Eric Schlosser, people were rejecting industrial food production, and movements sprang up in support of family farms, organics, artisanal food, craft breweries, and, of course, wine-making. (Wine being the original "craft" beverage business.) The movie Sideways, a funny, touching tribute to oenophilia, was a big hit around that time. And the wine market was skyrocketing, with sales up by nearly 50 percent over the previous decade.

As Baby Boomers aged, they were flocking to vineyards, mostly on the West Coast. *Instead of bringing the consumers to the grapes*, I thought, *why not bring the grapes to the consumers?* This was not an unheard-of concept. There were some urban wineries in California within a few hours of wine country, but nothing on the East Coast. Then there was Crushpad of San Francisco, launched the year before and doing great business by trucking the grapes in from nearby vineyards—so why shouldn't the concept work in New York? (Little did I know that, in a few years, Crushpad would be laid low by the 2008 recession.)

My idea was much different than Crushpad's, however, because from the very beginning, I envisioned music as a key part of the business. Every time I visited a winery, I would think: *This place is so cool. I want to stage a show here! Entertain around the beauty of the barrels.* Winemakers kept telling me how important hosting weddings were to the bottom line; some even made more from private events than from the wine itself!

I began to imagine how cool it would be to combine a wine-making facility with a music space and restaurant. Customers could smell the fermenting fruit and see the wooden French barrels while having dinner and watching a show, adding to the authenticity of the whole experience. But where would I get the grapes? I paid a visit to Hermann Wiemer, a great Riesling winemaker in the Finger Lakes region of upstate New York. He wanted to sell his winery and a mutual friend had introduced us, knowing that I'd become obsessed with making wine. Hermann needed someone to help him sell his business, and I agreed to help him write up a business plan.

As we talked, Herman made an offhand remark that spun me in a whole new direction. He mentioned that he could probably charge twice as much for a bottle of Pinot Noir made with grapes from Oregon's Willamette Valley as he could using fruit grown locally. My ears perked up. "I *love* Willamette Pinot Noir!" I said. Heck, I wanted to move my whole family to Oregon just to be near it. It's just too bad you can't ship those grapes....

Suddenly, a light bulb flashed on. How hard could it be? Excited, I did some calculations, and quickly realized that flying grapes in from the West Coast would never work—a typical order of 150 tons of fruit would require at least two Boeing 747s! But Hermann mentioned that California has been supplying grapes to the East Coast since the days of Prohibition and he knew of several wineries that got large deliveries of grapes in refrigerated trucks. If you keep the temperature at about 34 to 35 degrees Fahrenheit, the integrity of the fruit is hardly affected by the cross-country trip, which takes about five days. When the grapes arrived in Manhattan, they would have to be crushed immediately and the juice moved into giant stainless-steel tanks with glycol jackets to control the temperature as the fermenting process started. Because heat is created when the yeast in the skin converts the natural sugars into alcohol and carbon dioxide, the temperature in those tanks has to be carefully managed.

Many decisions would have to be made: From which vineyards should I buy the grapes? Separating the winery from the growers would actually leave us free to use only the best varietals, wherever they were—Pinot Noir from Sonoma and Willamette Valley; big Cabernets from Napa; Syrah from Paso Robles and Mendocino; maybe even go international, with Malbec grapes from Argentina. (Hmmm, that's in the Southern Hemisphere, cool—a second harvest season in springtime!) More decisions when you pour the wine into barrels: How much new oak versus old oak? New oak gives wine a bigger structure, though you'd have to wait longer for the tannins to emerge from the interaction between the fruit and the wood....

So many questions to contemplate! The complexity was not daunting; it was fascinating, like a puzzle begging to be put together. The challenge became even bigger when I realized that opening a music-and-wine venue was such a great idea, I wouldn't be satisfied with just one location—I'd want to scale it nationally, then internationally.

The excitement and endless possibilities were the fuel that kept me constantly thinking about this idea. As in my earliest days at the Knitting Factory, the ideas kept coming so often that it was hard to sleep. There was an endless to-do list of ways to expand, to get the word out. The sky's the limit! If it works in New York, why couldn't it work in any big city in the world? We could easily have thirty to forty locations in the US and Europe, maybe license more in Asia!

In April of 2006, I turned forty-four years old. With twenty years of experience, I was in my prime as an entrepreneur. I'd made lots of mistakes and now was my time to learn from them and make my comeback. I would do things right this time: Raise capital without losing control of my creation. Not get seduced by technology and make this a pure, live, sensory experience—no record company, no webcasts, and no freakin' Cones of Silence! I would build rooms that created a direct, intimate connection between the artists and their fans. I would venerate the musicians and treat them well. I would assemble a stellar management team, each member an expert and passionate about what they do. I would use all the cool and clever marketing tricks I could dream up. I would make the place relaxed and comfortable but add luxury elements like expensive Riedel stemware that heighten the taste of the wine, making it the kind of place I would love to go.

Finally, this was it—*Tabula rasa*, baby. Go big or go home.

The name of my new company popped into my head almost immediately. It had to clearly state who we are but be generic enough to work in any urban area, anywhere in the world. Plus, I love oxymorons, like "Knitting Factory"—they make you stop and think.

I had the perfect name: City Winery.

I got to work writing the business plan. Every winemaker knows that it's hard to make a great wine, but even harder to sell it. That's where music comes in. What more perfect way to bring thirsty customers to the watering hole? Fortunately, there is a big overlap between fans of music and wine, people who can think of no better way to spend an evening than listening to David Crosby or Shawn Colvin play a live set while sipping a Viognier from Paso Robles in an elegant Riedel glass after a sumptuous meal.

In putting together my business plan, I fell back on a rule I had established at the Knitting Factory: "Think in Excel, Present in Word." In other words, don't start by dreaming up a presentation in Microsoft Word because you haven't yet established the sustainability of the idea. Always start by crunching numbers in Excel—basically, how much money will be coming in, and how much going out. Create a business model, primitive or otherwise.

In my case, whether it's building a club or putting on a music festival, I always start by multiplying a predicted number of tickets by an estimated price to get my gross revenue. Then I tinker with those numbers—more or less capacity, higher or lower prices, food-and-beverage consumption estimates, sales and discounts, whatever—and Excel calculates the results automatically. Same with the cost side, which is usually a more predictable set of variables (except building contractors, whereby you need to take a real number and then add 50 percent for the ripoff factor). Then you can easily see whether you need to increase revenue or cut expenses to make the numbers work. Only then should you sit down and write out the business plan in Word, unleashing all your creativity and marketing savvy. Fine, go to PowerPoint (Keynote for us Apple heads) and razzle-dazzle with pictures, graphs, and whatever the fuck you think will help your pitch. But always start in Excel.

In going over the numbers, I realized that the perfect capacity for my venue would be 300 people. That would keep the place relatively small and cozy, but, with tickets at $50 to $75 apiece, still produce $15,000 to $22,500 per night at the box office, enough to book some exciting big-name artists. A capacity of 400 to 500 would be too big. Fans would no longer have eye contact with the musicians, killing that crucial sense of intimacy. I was adamant that most, if not all, of the ticket charge would go to the artists, who deserve it. This time, I didn't want there to be any question that I was there to serve them, not the other way around. Meanwhile, I could pay the staff and make profits for my investors using the old axiom of the theatrical film business: "The profits are in the popcorn." Just as movie-ticket sales go to the film producers and theaters earn their margins on concessions, I would extract the most revenue possible from the sale of food and high-margin wine and booze.

Restaurants and nightclubs tend to have slim profit margins—the reason so many fail in just a few years—so I needed another fail-safe revenue generator. That's where the custom wine-making came in. As I did my research—and talked extensively to Crushpad founder Michael Brill—I was candid about the fact that I was creating a music venue built around Crushpad's model of helping upscale customers create their own barrels of wine. The process would go like this: When customers signed up, we would learn their tastes and preferences and educate them to help them choose the exact blend of grapes, barrel type, duration of aging, and more. They could be as deeply involved or hands-off as they desired. In the end, they would get 250 bottles to drink or give away, with their name or logo prominently displayed on the label.

I crunched the numbers in Excel: If we could bring in 200 clients paying $10,000 per barrel, our gross would be $2 million. We would make another 100 barrels to serve to our customers at dinners and shows, for a total output of 300 barrels per year. Best of all, it would be like a futures setup: Since clients would pay up front for the barrel, it would give us much-needed cash flow in advance of making the wine. Since this was a luxury product, our customer base would come largely from Wall Street. Internally, I began calling it "Barrels for Bankers."

Immediately, I started talking up the idea to folks I knew on Wall Street. People at Lehman Brothers would tell their friends at Bear Stearns, who would tell others at Morgan Stanley. With the stock market red hot, money was no object and my customer list multiplied rapidly. When I asked them, "Would you like a so-so Cabernet at about thirty-five dollars a bottle or the best Napa Cab possible for forty-five dollars?" they would always ask for the best. And when I said, "Would you like your barrel to have new French oak for a thousand bucks or American oak for four hundred?" they would sniff and say, "French oak, of course."

Once my business plan was done, I put it into a wooden binder made of thin plywood, with the words "City Winery" engraved on it. I wanted it to stand out among all the other business proposals that cluttered people's desks. The wood was symbolic of the wine barrels, the tactile approach our company was taking, the classiness of the project. In contrast to my internet days, I loved that everything now was tangible and real.

By late 2007, I was ready to start raising money. I sent the wooden binder to about thirty people I thought might be interested—rich friends, people I knew who invested, friends of friends. I networked hard and did a lot of schmoozing at school fundraisers, wine dinners, the exclusive Soho House hotel/members club, anywhere I could work a crowd.

This time, I would not make the same mistake I made with the Knitting Factory, when I allowed the Vulture Capitalists to buy preferred shares and lost control. This time, I would gather *lots* of investors willing to put up smaller amounts, so nobody would have disproportionate influence—and *everyone* would have common shares, so this time, the playing field would be even.

Soon, I was reminded what a chicken-and-egg situation it is to start a business. No landlord would sign a lease unless I had investors, but investors are loath to put money up without a lease. When I tried to get potential investors excited about a space I found on West 33rd Street near the Hudson River, an even better option became available—a 21,000-square-foot space on Varick Street in Tribeca, near the Holland Tunnel. I had to quickly switch gears and tell the investors that *this* was the ideal place to open City Winery.

Another chicken-and-egg scenario played out when several potential investors expressed interest but none of them wanted to be the first, or "lead" investor. They wanted to follow others who had already negotiated the price of their shares and, thus, the overall value of the company. So I asked one of the interested investors who was a friend to do me a solid: Write me the first check, which I can use to entice the others to follow. He did. One investment led to another, and in the spring of 2008, I was able to assemble a total of ten partners, including myself. Each of us put up $150,000, for a total capitalization of $1.5 million. It was amazing because the amount per investor I was able to negotiate happened to be exactly how much I had extracted when I sold my stake in the Knitting Factory.

I knew $1.5 million would not be enough to get a winery, restaurant, and music club up and running by opening night on New Year's Eve 2008—that would take another $3 million to $5 million. But, at least, it would allow me to get the ball rolling by signing a lease for the Varick Street location. It was a scary moment. In May, I signed a fifteen-year lease for a first-year rent of $400,000 (and that was at a discount). Over the years, I had learned that, after you've done everything possible to mitigate your risk, at some point, you just have to say, "Fuck it, I'm diving in." Sure, it takes chutzpah, but nobody should be an entrepreneur without having tons of that in your DNA.

Construction began. We needed to complete the winery first, so we could accept fruit in early September.

Remembering that magical moment when I met Lou Reed while the Knitting Factory on Leonard Street was under construction, I decided to hold a series of "Hard Hat Dinners" for potential investors, artists, journalists, talent agents, and other dignitaries amid the sawdust, sheet rock, and dangling wires. I realized that it's exciting for people to feel they are getting in on the ground floor of something special as it's being created. It makes them feel like an insider receiving an exclusive peek inside a hot new venture, like an embedded reporter in a war zone. I started with a small staff, including an assistant, graphic designer, and a tall Israeli intern. We washed wine glasses from a single basin sink, spread out some tablecloths, and tried to keep everything clean while the workers made a huge mess.

The Hard Hat Dinners were a success. Eventually I raised another $2.5 million—plus a loan of $750,000—from thirty-three investors, each putting in small amounts ranging from $25,000 to $200,000. My total capitalization was just under $5 million. Clearly, they were betting on me—not Michael Dorf the winemaker, but the music impresario and hospitality guy who had created the whole package. That was flattering but also hugely daunting. Could I pull it off?

By late summer, things looked good. Eighty customers had signed up for our Barrels for Bankers custom wine-making program, which would bring in nearly $1 million in revenue. With 120 more, we would be at full capacity. I was jazzed. To make sure our wine would be of the highest quality, I hired the superstar winemaker David Lecomte, a Frenchman with degrees from universities in Burgundy and Montpellier who had worked for many top wineries in the US and France.

Trucks carrying the first shipments of the most expensive grapes in the world were scheduled to pull up to our curb in September—seventy-five tons of fruit from eleven sources, including ten tons of Cabernet from the famed Napa grower Larry Bettinelli and eight tons of Pinot Noir from the Bacigalupi family, one of the top vineyards in the Russian River area of California.

I had no idea, of course, that, just as I was staging my phoenix-like comeback from the dot-com debacle, I was getting caught up in another bubble—this time, created by a housing mania and Wall Street venality. On September 15, 2008—the same day our first grapes arrived—Lehman Brothers filed for bankruptcy. The news was suddenly filled with talk of a global economic collapse. It was one of those shocking moments, like 9/11, when people in my neighborhood—especially on Wall Street—seemed to be walking around shell-shocked, like zombies. Though I kept trying to raise money, investors were now nearly impossible to find. Even worse, most of those eighty customers in our Barrels for Bankers program disappeared. Many were suddenly out of work. Even those who could still afford to spend $10,000 on custom-made wine were embarrassed to let anyone know it. "I just can't flaunt this now," they whispered.

My whole enterprise seemed be going up in smoke. What to do? Let's see, if the wine-making collapses, maybe we can just call ourselves a concert hall/restaurant with a great wine list? But does anybody still have money to go out for dinner and a show?

By October, we were still $1 million short of what we needed to open on New Year's Eve. But having spent so much of my investors' money, I couldn't pull the plug now. We were already booking shows and selling tickets. I had no choice but to power through and hope for the best—keep the wine operation going, sell tickets, use all available credit, postpone paying some vendors—whatever it takes to get the place open and start bringing in some cash.

Fortunately, I had the great Joan Osborne appearing on New Year's Eve—exactly the kind of artist I knew my customer base would love. She sold out quickly. The main features of our ticketing system that we had built from scratch—being able to select your seat so you don't have to come early and wait in line, and our paid membership "Vinofile" program that lets you avoid service fees—all were immediately popular. People jumped at the chance to see Joan up close on a big holiday night out.

As for the artists, I saw City Winery as my chance to make amends for the way I had neglected them at the end of the Knitting Factory run, when I got so wrapped up in the technology and pleasing investors that music became a mere commodity. I invested in a state-of-the-art Meyer sound system, made sure the dressing room was comfortable, and allowed the artists to wine and dine with friends. I was almost overdoing it to make up for being so stingy in the past, just trying my best to make them feel at home.

My biggest regret was that I couldn't book all the fantastic musicians I knew and loved, some of them very good friends, because I knew they would not be able to fill a 300-seat club. So I was happy years later to open nearby 100- to 150-seat "satellite" venues like The Loft at City Winery and City Vineyard to accommodate those artists and their fans. A few years earlier, I had also tried to patch things up with John Zorn by helping him set up the Stone, a performance space in the East Village. He needed help navigating some architectural issues and legal and bureaucratic obstacles, so I did whatever I could, in a brotherly way, and was glad to help him create an important venue for avant-garde artists.

It was a mad rush to finish construction of City Winery before New Year's Eve, and we didn't get our official temporary occupancy permit from the city until December 29. Then I had to run up to Harlem to show the document to the State Liquor Authority, which had approved our license but could not issue it until our space was certified by the city. Since our wine was still in barrels, I then had to run back to order wine and beer and spirits to be delivered in time for the show.

December 31 arrived. I was a bundle of nerves as Joan came onto the stage to do her sound check. Seeing my distress, she gave me the big hug I never forgot. Instantly, I felt better. When the show started—Joan fronting a killer five-piece band—the crowd loved it. The vibe was so warm and magical that night, I felt foolish for once believing I could replicate such an intimate experience all over the planet with just some video cameras connected to the internet. If my career was about anything, it was this—creating a cozy space for a musician to open up her heart and soul to her fans, who are eager to reciprocate. It's that simple, and that beautiful.

But I also had to worry about keeping a roof over our heads. I scanned the room to see whether people were buying enough popcorn to keep my little movie theater running. One couple, I noticed, was drinking a $250 bottle of Ridge

Monte Bello—ironically, made by David Tate, whose excess Cabernet grapes had gotten me hooked on wine-making in the first place. Later, the couple ordered another bottle. "Yes!" I thought, "We're gonna make it!" When they left, I sauntered over and glanced at the check to revel in my success and noticed that the server had mistakenly billed them for another Ridge wine—a Zinfandel listed at thirty-five dollars a bottle. Oy! That thirty-five dollars didn't come close to covering the hundred-dollar wholesale cost of the Monte Bello—and they bought two bottles!

City Winery might be a great idea, but our execution definitely needed some work.

In the months that followed, booking the club with great musicians was no problem. Producing the Carnegie Hall tribute concerts had introduced me to some amazing artists and their agents and managers, so I was able to bring in folks like Steve Earle, Suzanne Vega, Marc Cohen, and Patti Smith. It was incredibly gratifying when Steve Earle later told me why he plays at City Winery.

"Tell you the truth, it's not actually about the club," he said. "And it's not about the wine, because I don't drink anymore. It's about you. Because you always gave a fuck about music."

With lineups like that, filling the club every night was relatively easy, which surprised me a bit, because there's lots of competition in New York for people's entertainment dollars. We started with some conventional advertising, but soon built up such an extensive email list from our website and ticketing system that we eventually eliminated advertising altogether. And the artists themselves brought their own followings. Another big factor was our respect for people's precious time. They could see the show and have a great dinner at the same place, knowing what seat or table they had reserved online—even eat while watching the act if they wanted to, which allowed them to show up at 8 p.m. after working late or putting their kids to bed. And we have never had a drink or food minimum, so you can just drink free water if you want—though not many people do, since the great food and wine are so tempting.

In many ways, we were an immediate success, with sold-out houses nearly every night. But, by March of 2009, we were still a million dollars in debt, with no new investors in sight. Every day, the question nagged at me: Are we going to make it?

One day, I got a call from a collection agency for a company that had sold us wine barrels and now wanted the $50,000 we owed them. "Michael, you are married to Sarah Connors, your children are Zachary, Eli, and Sophia, we know your home street address, and we will hold you personally accountable if you don't pay off your entire debt within ten days," he said. "Believe me, you can't even imagine the things we are capable of."

It wasn't the only call like that I got. We owed money to dozens of vendors and now my family was at risk. Freaking out, with the economy still tanking, I decided to take out a loan to settle those debts. It would take me two years to pay off and I had to give up some equity, but I had no choice.

Meanwhile, City Winery's entire financial structure was still reeling from the demise of my Barrels for Bankers program, a crucial part of our business plan. Without that projected $2 million in revenue, we were just an ordinary restaurant/music club, in debt from startup costs and trying to survive with razor-thin profit margins. We had three hundred barrels of wine, made from painfully expensive California and Oregon grapes, just sitting in our basement. We could use about one hundred of those barrels to bottle and sell on the premises, but that still left two hundred barrels of surplus, and only twenty-five had been bought and paid for. "Where are my one hundred and seventy-five customers who are going to take this wine off my hands and save the company?" I wailed to anyone who would listen.

My brother Josh had a different question. "When was the last time you tasted that wine?" he said. It had been months, I told him—probably back in December when we transferred the wine from our stainless-steel tanks into the wooden barrels. "Well, go down there with David," he said, referring to my ace winemaker, Monsieur Lecomte, "and do a tasting to take your mind off your troubles. Come on, it's amazing wine!"

Josh had to practically push me out of the office. Finally, I realized he was right. *Why should everybody else enjoy the fruits of my hard work? I want some too!*

So David and I went down there and started sampling. Inserting a long, phallic-looking glass "thief" into the bung-hole at the top of the barrels, we went around the room with our Riedel glasses tasting the wine. David deftly spit into a drain on the floor—the dude can send a steady stream into a bucket from ten feet away without spilling a drop—and didn't swallow much. I, on the other hand, swallowed most of mine. My spitting style was more machine-gun than laser and soaked everything within five feet of my mouth, including my shirt and pants.

As we tasted, David gave me another of his master classes in the nuances of wine-making, describing in mesmerizing detail the magic of the barrels—new oak versus old, French versus American, heavily toasted versus lightly toasted—and why it's important to know from which forests the various barrel-makers, known as coopers, are pulling wood. That's why, with eight different coopers, fifteen vineyards producing ten varieties of grapes, and subtle differences in aging, each of those three hundred barrels were astonishingly different.

"But all of them are fantastic!" I said, soaking wet, draining another sip.

By now, I was a bit sloshed. "My God, this is delicious," I said, holding onto a rack of barrels to keep my balance. "David, you are really good! This wine is ready to sell! Come on, we have to move it! If each barrel has over a thousand glasses of wine, dude, at fifteen dollars a glass, that's fifteen thousand dollars. Now just multiply that by two hundred and seventy-five barrels..."

At that moment, I was too elated to do the calculations, but I knew it was a lot of money—over $4 million, in fact. We were sitting on a gold mine! "Screw the bottling process; that'll cost too much money," I said. The solution was clear: "Let's just tap these motherfuckers! We need to get this into our customers' bloodstreams NOW!"

"Michael, you are such a stupid American," David said in his thick French accent. "If you put gas pressure on a wooden barrel, it's going to blow up."

But he had another idea: "What I have seen done, not very often in this country, maybe a little more in Europe, but still very rare, is this: Move the wine into a stainless-steel keg and then tap the keg. Just like you would beer."

"Really? Would that work?"

"Scientifically, it should, but I'm not so certain customers will be into it," David said.

Today, the buzz word is "pivot," but I would say it was more "necessity breeds invention." We immediately started selling wine on tap. I came up with the phrase, "We are vessel agnostic—barrel or glass, who cares?" When the wine was ready, we poured it into fifteen- and thirty-gallon stainless steel kegs. Immediately, the economic advantages became clear: We did not have to pay for thousands of bottles, corks, labels, cardboard boxes, and hours of staff time. We didn't have to waste leftover wine in bottles; the wine can last indefinitely in the kegs, thanks to a neutral argon gas used to preserve it. And it was far more environmentally friendly because we conserved all those glass bottles and labels and didn't have to use the sulfite preservative found in bottled wine.

Customers loved it too. Eventually, we designed City Winery interiors to make it look like the taps were coming out of old wine barrels mounted in the wall—a kind of classic European look that felt more authentic. To my astonishment, the tap wine sold like crazy, far more than we had been selling by the bottle. It was exciting for customers to know that their wine was being poured directly from a fully functional winery they could see, through glass windows, right on the premises.

On busy nights, we began moving nearly one thousand glasses of wine, and the profit margins were significantly higher than if we had sold the wine by the barrel. Today, we still have about thirty to forty clients a year who make their own wine, but my original business plan of having two-thirds of our wine sales coming from custom barrels has been turned upside down: today, fully 70 percent of our wine sales come by the glass, consumed on site.

Adding up those numbers made me realize, for the first time, that City Winery was going to make it. In fact, our net profit during that first year was higher than I ever achieved over a whole decade at the Knitting Factory.

It was especially satisfying to hear experts raving about our wine. "The wines are really well made," Randall Grahm of Bonny Doon Vineyard told *Wine Spectator* magazine in 2009. "He's got a talented winemaker." Jean-Luc Le Dû, the legendary sommelier and wine merchant, called our wines "pretty wonderful," citing our Zinfandel, in particular. I even got Joe Bastianich, the partner of chef Mario Batali, to come in and talk to me about our wines, and he loved the way we were selling them—fresh from a tap, with no sulfites. It started to get very exciting. Our extensive wine list won awards from Wine Spectator and we hosted wine tastings by Kevin Zraly, author of the best-selling book *Windows on the World Complete Wine Course.*

Eric Asimov of *The New York Times*, commending our lineup of artists and winemakers, put it simply: "I've got a lot of reasons to want to hang out at City Winery."

Stumbling upon the keg solution was dumb luck, I knew, but it was the kind that can only happen when you make a leap of faith. By 2010, our revenues had reached $10 million a year with healthy profits, and I was ready to make another leap. As the ground beneath us began to feel more solid, it was time to think about the next step: How can I scale the concept into a national chain without losing the magic of the original?

Fifteen years earlier, I thought the internet would let me scale the intimate experiences in my club all over the world, cheaply and quickly. Now I knew better. That was fool's gold. This time, I would use atoms, not bits. To replicate what made City Winery special, I would have to construct each link in the chain slowly, methodically, maybe even exhaustingly, one brick-and-mortar establishment, one well-trained manager, one skillful server, one barrel of wine, one mind-blowing show at a time.

6

Scaling Intimacy Is Not an Oxymoron

Have you noticed how companies often hide behind technology—websites, apps, phone trees, etc.—to avoid having to interact with you, the customer, on a personal level? How about when you can't find a salesperson to help you in a store? Frustrating, right? These companies are failing one of the fundamental tasks of any business: to create a sense of intimacy that makes you feel cared for, valued, and respected.

Some would say that's simply a function of size or efficiency. How can a big company extend such a personal touch to all its customers? Isn't "scaling intimacy" an oxymoron, like an elevated subway or meatless meatballs? In a word, no. Creating a deep connection to *all* your customers as a company grows may not be easy, but it's hardly impossible. Indeed, it can be richly rewarding for everyone involved.

Take Starbucks, for example. It scales intimacy in many ways across its worldwide chain of 28,000 stores. What I especially appreciate is its attention to sensory detail. Starbucks uses muted colors, recessed lighting, wood finishes, and just the right music at a low volume to create a cozy, ultra-relaxing place to hang out with friends or get some work done. Handwritten names on cups, instituted under then-CEO Howard Schultz, helps each coffee house feel like it's the only one.

Steve Jobs also grokked this concept well, something you notice the moment you unwrap your iPhone: The package is a triumph of minimalist design that's nearly as magnificent as the device inside. Apple's packaging designers tested hundreds of boxes of various sizes, shapes, and angles before settling on one that's not only aesthetically pleasing, but intuitively useful. Why go to so much trouble over a silly box? It's all to elicit a tactile, emotional response that makes you feel well cared for and even more excited about your new phone, computer, or watch.

Another company that scales intimacy beautifully is Union Square Hospitality Group, creators of Shake Shack. Founder Danny Meyer, the great restaurateur whom I'll talk about later in this chapter, does it by creating a culture of what he calls "enlightened hospitality." That simply means focusing intensely on how the delivery of a product or service makes a customer feel. "Virtually nothing else is as important as how one is made to feel in any business transaction," Danny says. To achieve enlightened hospitality, he treats his staff extremely well and trains them deeply in the art of making customers feel special. The physical space is welcoming and fun, with smart touches like open kitchens placed in front rather than hidden in the back. And customers notice that he uses only the best ingredients, just as he does in his legendary fine-dining establishments. Shake Shack now has more than 200 locations around the world, with lots more on the way. CEO Randy Garutti articulates the company's approach to growth this way: "The bigger we get, the smaller we need to act."

Great advice, but easier said than done—as I discovered when I tried to replicate the magic of City Winery beyond our first home in New York City.

As I thought about expanding, one city kept coming back to me as our perfect second location: Chicago. As a Midwesterner, I understood the city's culture well. Just a ninety-minute drive from my native Milwaukee, Chicago has always been sophisticated like New York but more homey and down-to-earth. A high-end winery/restaurant/concert space with a cozy, intimate feel seemed like a natural fit. Like many cities, Chicago has a great music scene with several good clubs about our size but none with a decent restaurant, and certainly none making wine on the premises. I commissioned no surveys and had no data saying Chicago would work. But even when a well-known promoter took me to an old-school steakhouse and told me I was crazy—the city was already overpopulated with music venues, he insisted—something in my gut told me it would be a home run.

I started looking hard for a space in 2010, two years after opening in New York, traveling to Chicago often to survey neighborhoods. Hoping to stay out of the more expensive and predictable nightlife areas north of downtown, I explored the West Loop. The area had lots of the kind of historic brick buildings I love—in this case, former food warehouses—and was starting to develop a culinary reputation. I found a 32,000-square-foot property at Randolph Street and Racine Avenue, selling for $2.5 million. That seemed like a good deal, given that the neighborhood was on the rise. (I was right; after the Nobu Hotel, Soho House, and corporate offices for Google and McDonald's moved in, our once-dilapidated building is now worth at least six times what we paid for it.)

It was important that our second location not feel like a cookie-cutter knockoff or be seen as one of those "theme" venues like Hard Rock Cafe, House of Blues, or B.B. King's that can veer toward the tacky and touristy. After House of Blues was bought by Live Nation, the biggest concert producer in the world, it moved from smaller capacities to large rooms for over a thousand people, erasing the original design intimacy created by founder Isaac Tigrett that differentiated it from other venues. While there was something to be learned from each of those companies—and I've met many of the players along the way—none of them offered a model for what we were trying to do.

Being a pioneer made it a challenge to convince new investors that expanding City Winery beyond Manhattan would work. But holding Hard Hat Dinners in the new space got a bunch of them excited, and our success in New York was compelling enough to attract twenty-three more partners who put up $3 million to fund our Chicago expansion.

When we began construction, I had yet to coin the phrase "scaling intimacy" but knew the feeling I wanted to create in the new space. Fascinated by construction since I was a teenager building rec rooms—and later expanding the Knitting Factory multiple times—I always like to begin with the physical plant itself: the building and materials used to renovate it.

Our buildings in New York and Chicago were both built in the late 1800s and had the texture and authenticity of real brick and old wooden beams, something that's hard to replicate with new building products. Companies that use fake plastic bricks and super-durable vinyl flooring that sort of look like real wood aren't fooling anybody and make the room feel cheap. Sometimes that's better than other design choices, but there is something about the irregularities, the distress and age of older materials that creates a certain warmth—and, for a music venue like ours, makes for much better acoustics.

I got especially excited about using old barrel staves for our front bars, walls, and some ceiling treatments. Wine-stained on the inside and beat up on the outside, they created a classy but homey look while the fact that they were "reclaimed" or "reused" materials added the subtle dimension of purpose by demonstrating our environmental consciousness. Mounting barrels on the walls with taps poking out made it clear the wine was coming directly from our winery. We offered a selection of fourteen of our tap wines in the restaurant and five in the performance venue, in addition to an extensive bottle list.

Since our first venue in New York was kind of slapped together, Chicago became the much improved 2.0 version, giving me a chance to learn from my mistakes. One new feature was a barrel room behind a glass wall with our stacks of French oak barrels clearly visible from nearly anywhere in the club. It was a gorgeous look, inspired by some of the world's great barrel rooms, like Opus One Winery in Napa; Château Margaux and Château Pichon Longueville Baron in Bordeaux; Bodega Catena Zapata and Bodegas Salentein in Mendoza, Argentina. Each of those rooms is such a rare combination of brilliant architecture and exquisite taste that just entering them can overwhelm your senses.

Lighting was another critical component in creating an intimate atmosphere, especially for a nighttime business like ours. I wanted a soft, candlelit effect, using dimmable LED lighting. Our hanging lamps come from an old friend from college named Liz Galbraith, an amazing designer whose handmade paper lighting creates just the right vibe in all our locations.

All those sublime touches would mean nothing, of course, if we treated our guests with the same level of suspicion, even aggression, they encounter at stadium concerts, sporting events and some smaller clubs—being patted down by security, scanned with wands, and ordered to produce identification. That's the opposite of the feeling we want to create, so we came up with a paperless ticketing system that requires you only to give your name at the door. A greeter quickly looks you up on a tablet and escorts you to your table; if you are a Vinofile member, we will already know your favorite wine and other preferences, creating the kind of familiarity you would get from an old-school maître d' at your regular restaurant—even in a growing chain like ours that accommodates 3,000 customers around the country every night.

I could go on and on about the endless details I enjoy obsessing over to achieve a cozy, comfortable feel in our clubs, everything from the quality of the bass amps in our sound system to the stemware—always Riedel, the best glass on the market, carefully designed to steer the wine toward areas of the tongue that lead to the utmost pleasure. Not all companies have the patience for that level of precision. Live Nation doesn't seem to worry too much about what kind of paper cups it offers at its stadium rock concerts, but it should. I'm convinced that maximizing sensory pleasure will become a crucial differentiator between competing brands as our lives are increasingly dominated by devices that pull us away from the physical world.

As our Chicago club took shape, I was extremely careful not to make the same mistake I made with the Los Angeles Knitting Factory—setting an ambitious opening date, booking talent, selling tickets, and then having to cancel shows and refund money because of construction delays. Opening two months later than scheduled in LA cost us a ton of money and generated the kind of customer anger and negative publicity that no new business should have to endure during what should be a joyous occasion.

This time, we got it mostly right. Our Chicago club opened on schedule on August 15, 2012. Mayor Rahm Emanuel was there—in sharp contrast to New York, where I couldn't even get Hizzoner Mike Bloomberg to respond to my invitations. The place looked magnificent. Guests were handed Champagne as they arrived and nibbled on hand-crafted appetizers. I was psyched to have the great comedian Lewis Black, then a weekly guest on Jon Stewart's *Daily Show*, appearing for the first of a sold-out five-night run. When the *Chicago Tribune* described us as "warm, woody, with hints of Sonoma, but still recognizably metropolitan," I knew we had hit the mark. That was exactly what we were going for—wine country in the city.

Going forward, the trick was to create that same relaxed California/Italian vibe in every location without making each venue feel like a sterile reproduction of some pristine ideal. Bob Gruen, the great rock-and-roll photographer, later came to speak to our staff at an offsite meeting and used a great metaphor to sum up our approach: His photographs should never be judged by their sharpness or focus, he said, but about how well he captures vibe. The image might be fuzzy, but that's irrelevant if it captures the moment. So, while everything might not be perfect at your local City Winery—the heat a little high, the food a little cold—even those imperfections, if presented well and with a smile, can create a homespun feeling of relaxed intimacy with a crowd of 300 strangers. As Voltaire put it, "The best is the enemy of the good."

Of course, that's no excuse for lousy food or bad service. I guess things got a little too fuzzy on opening night when it took some diners over ninety minutes to get their food— "And even then, the sweet potato fries were lukewarm," complained the *Chicago Tribune*. Embarrassed, I immediately emailed guests to apologize and offered them all a free dinner or two-for-one tickets to a future show.

Sensing a weakness, the food press pounced. A month later, *Time Out Chicago*'s Julia Kramer wrote a scathing review, giving us one star: "How much longer are we supposed to wait for this New York import to get its act together?" she groused. Though she enjoyed the wine, she wrote that the service was "borderline hopeless," her flank steak was dry, her spiced walnuts tasted "the way paint smells" and her molten lava cake was overcooked.

That was painful, and I took it personally. In response, I published a letter to Kramer in a full-page ad in the next issue to apologize and ask for patience as we "get our sea legs." I fired our chef, brought in our stellar New York executive chef Andres Barrera, and we upped our game tremendously. Some customers who gave us bad marks that first week became devoted fans and, after months of hard work, our Yelp reviews started showing "vast improvement."

Within two years, our Chicago location became a power-house, bringing in sales nearly equal to New York. Today, it is one of our top performers. It's hard to pinpoint precisely what made it so successful after that rocky start. This being my first attempt at expanding City Winery, I was deeply involved from the beginning, personally hiring the first ten employees who formed our core team, many of whom are still with us, and trying to plant the seeds of our company's DNA directly into the new soil, stressing everything from training to company culture to best practices. I was also fortunate to have a strong bench in New York to pull from to fill top positions. Some of the Chicago team members they trained would later help open subsequent locations, creating a virtuous and self-perpetuating cycle.

As involved as I was, my team was so good that I did not have to micromanage them, allowing me to soon cut back my visits to once a month. They understood the culture we were trying to establish, and a kind of friendly rivalry developed between New York and Chicago about which team could run a better operation and generate more sales. When New York employees started saying about an operational issue, "What would Chicago do?" it annoyed our Varick Street managers to no end.

Chicago also attracted many young, ambitious team members who wanted to grow in the entertainment/hospitality business and saw our company as a great vehicle for that. Our wine program offers a good example of the kind of healthy ambition I'm talking about. In all our venues, we want our people to know everything about wine—not just how to serve it and talk to customers about it, but also how we actually *make* the wine, where the grapes come from, the soil, the varietals, etc., all the nuances that make us special. Our Chicago wine director, Rachel Speckan, took things even further by creating an internal wine course to elevate our staff's knowledge. She also hosted an international sommelier program that allowed our team to participate. The results were spectacular: At one point, we had eighteen certified sommeliers in Chicago, twice as many as any other restaurant in the city. Today, over a hundred of our servers at that location proudly wear a pin on their lapel earned for passing our wine program.

As City Winery expanded and our staffing swelled, I was forced to confront my strengths and weaknesses as a manager. I turned fifty the year Chicago opened, so I was no longer the restless punk who started the Knitting Factory, where some employees felt I pushed them too hard and did not pay them enough. There was probably some truth to those complaints—though it's also true that I paid myself less than everyone else at the Knit, and then only after everybody else got their checks. In fact, I probably made an average of $10,000 a year in my first decade there. At City Winery, I knew I needed to take some of the edge off my high expectations by finding ways to inspire people so they came to work jazzed—looking forward to who is playing that night, wondering if they will meet the artists, hoping there will be a tasting to learn more about wine, and seeking out the general manager to explore ideas about hospitality.

I also learned how important it was to hire great people and then leave them alone to do their jobs. The one who taught me that was Ed Greer. A musician and carpenter from Ireland, Ed started as a sound guy at the Knitting Factory, moved up to head bartender, and eventually became a tremendously loyal and trusted manager who allowed me to take some nights off, knowing the club was in good hands. At City Winery, he was one of my first hires and a big key to our ability to scale, because I knew he would keep things running smoothly while I was off searching for new locations. Ed taught me it was okay to trust someone else's decision-making ability and hear "no" to some of my wackier ideas. (I used to call him the "voice of reason.") Thanks to people like Ed, I'm now able to delegate to folks who are more competent than me—at everything from wine-making and waiting tables to running a kitchen and managing operations. (Sales and marketing is the exception, since that's second nature to me; but, even there, I'm happy to defer to others with great ideas.) I've always been proud to say that, after all these years in the nightclub business, I still don't know what goes into a cocktail. I couldn't fix you a Manhattan to save my life. I've always had great bartenders to do that.

When it comes to pay, City Winery certainly can't afford hedge fund salaries, but we pay the best we possibly can and try to make sure that our ownership group is not taking home exploitive profits. I add perks whenever possible, from yoga and SoulCycle classes to the turkeys we give out at Thanksgiving. The turkey giveaway is something my grandfather Sol used to do at the Milwaukee Biscuit Company, where employees were treated like family. We just add a modern twist by asking people to provide a short story and photo of their meal, so we can share it on social media. Some people love doing that and others couldn't care less. That's fine, I'm just trying to do whatever I can to create a family atmosphere where everyone feels valued and respected.

From the moment I first conceived of City Winery, I knew I would have to not only create a strong culture in New York but find a way to replicate it across the dozens, if not hundreds, of locations I wanted to open eventually. I had no illusions that this would be easy. In fact, this may well be the hardest, and most crucial, part of building a large, sustainable company. Mindful of Peter Drucker's maxim that "Culture eats strategy for breakfast," I put in a disproportionate amount of time and energy into thinking about how to create a powerful motivational structure to create and perpetuate a great company culture.

The main mechanism for doing this, I decided, would be an annual offsite meeting for managers called Basecamp. The name was important. I did not want to call it a "retreat," as many companies do—that sounds like "getting away from it all" and going *backwards*. Instead, these events should move the company *forward* and give us a chance to engage more deeply with our work and each other. Since I'm a rock climber and mountain guy, Basecamp seemed like the perfect metaphor for what we would be doing at these events—regrouping in a safe place with our team; assessing our strengths and weaknesses; clarifying our goals as we struggle to reach the summit; developing and reaffirming the principles that will get us there; and making sure everybody is drinking the same Kool-Aid (or Petite Syrah, as it were)—goals that become far more challenging as a company gets larger.

Our first Basecamp was small, held in 2011 when we still had a single location. We went to Minnewaska State Park in upstate New York, did some rope climbing, and gathered for a whiteboard discussion on the cliff rocks that resulted in the creation of our mission statement, which we still use today: "To provide a gathering place that is the best combination of culinary and cultural arts in a beautiful and comfortable setting that celebrates life and provides pleasure to all who enter."

Our second Basecamp the next year was larger and more sophisticated because now we had Chicago, too. About thirty of us went to Miami. On that trip, I splurged and put everybody up at the Ritz-Carlton for two nights because I wanted the team to see how great it makes you feel when the receptionist comes out from behind the desk to show you to your room, a lovely gesture replicated in more than ninety Ritz-Carltons worldwide every day. Now *that's* scaling intimacy. The theme of Basecamp that year was the culture of innovation at Apple. We imagined how Steve Jobs and his company would define our business and view our attempts to "think different" with a winery/restaurant/concert venue chain that nobody had ever attempted before.

The next year, we went to Puerto Rico, where we created a team-building exercise by staging a Top Chef-like cook-off: Chicago versus New York. The two teams created a multicourse meal using a pile of ingredients and kitchen equipment and whatever they could find on the beach. Our art directors made the menus, the beverage directors whipped up cocktails, and the rest of team argued about what to cook, how to make it delicious, and how to present it beautifully. The whole thing was a gas, and we all shared in the spoils when it turned into a beach party. Chicago won, but it was close. Afterward, I got many thank-you notes from managers saying the bonding experience truly helped make their operations run better.

By 2013, with Chicago running smoothly, I was eager to launch our next City Winery. Since I'm not as competent or interested in the minutiae of running the venues themselves, my job was strategic responsibilities: identifying new locations, building them out, and raising capital. And I was good at it. With our two clubs bringing in a total of $20 million in annual revenue, I was beginning to think this scaling thing was easy.

How wrong I was. After seriously considering Los Angeles or one of the big East Coast cities, I decided instead to establish a beachhead in California wine country by opening in the city of Napa. Some of the appeal was emotional—I just love Napa and its great wine community—and part was strategic: I thought it would improve our relationship with the vineyards and winemakers, giving us access to more and better grapes, and let us connect with the more than five million tourists who flock to America's best-known wine country every year, a crowd that exactly fits our demographic profile. As an indoor venue for private parties, we would be insulated from California's crazy weather events (well, not earthquakes, as we had our opening year. Oy!) and provide an alternative to outdoor wineries that were not legally allowed to host private events like weddings.

At the time, there was a lot of development happening downtown, and the beautiful old Napa Valley Opera House, circa 1880, was struggling to attract audiences for its theatrical and musical productions. I fell in love with the old building and we committed to spend $3 million to renovate it only a few years after the legendary Mondavi wine family had spent over $10 million making it seismically safe. After raising money from investors, we put in a real kitchen to create a full restaurant on the ground floor, installed a professional-grade sound system, and pulled out the 450 fixed raked auditorium seats to create an open floor for our usual oak tables and chairs. I decided we should not actually make wine there, figuring it made no sense to compete against the all-star wineries of Napa. Instead, we would have a fantastic wine list featuring our innovative and environmentally friendly tap system using wine from more than a dozen local partners, many of whom had never served tap wine before.

On one level, Napa was a big success from the moment we opened in April of 2014. This being a small city of less than 80,000, we had to work extra hard on marketing to bring in the tourists and residents of the region, but it paid off: For the first few months, we sold out nearly every night with our usual high-caliber lineup of artists, including Bruce Cockburn, Lewis Black, and Los Lobos, along with emerging local talent.

But we made one huge, dumb mistake: Nobody was drinking. After a long day of touring wineries and tasting Napa's great Cabernets and Chardonnays, the last thing our customers wanted to do was order wine. They wanted to hydrate with water! (Maybe, at best, sparkling water.) With a customer base that wanted to toss back free glasses of water instead of seventy-five-dollar bottles of wine, Napa did only about 25 percent of the sales volume of New York or Chicago in the all-important, high-margin category of alcohol. Then there were the dozens of friends in the wine industry who came excited to see the shows but brought their own wine. We couldn't very well charge these rock stars of the wine world corkage fees. An expectation also emerged among industry folks that samples from our extensive wine list were on the house, followed all too rarely by an order for a paid glass or bottle. Making up the lost revenue with private parties didn't work, either. It turns out the towns rarely enforced those zoning laws against outdoor events at wineries.

All in all, Napa was a bust. We closed at the end of 2015, less than two years after opening. My then-sixteen-year-old son Eli summed up perfectly how we screwed up: "Dad, there's a reason it's called City Winery!" For all its charms, Napa is actually more like a small rural town, one already chock-full of wineries. Smite forehead: D'oh!

Closing Napa was a huge disappointment. The good news is that it remains our only failure. Over the next few years, we would have our share of crises, but our next four locations—Nashville, Atlanta, Boston, and Washington, D.C.—are now running smoothly and turning healthy profits.

In Nashville, which opened in September of 2014, just five months after Napa, we struggled at first, because the neighborhood was still a bit sketchy. We bought and renovated a 30,000-square-foot warehouse but some people were afraid to walk to our venue from the main strip, and parking was difficult. Since then, several new hotels have opened nearby—Jimmy Buffett is opening his Margaritaville Hotel just a block away—and we fixed some managerial issues. Now it's exciting to see Nashville humming, hitting our sales goals even in a famous music capital with no shortage of concert venues.

The challenge in Atlanta was not finding a great location. It was clear that a vibrant commercial and residential development called Ponce City Market was perfect. The problem was the rent was too high and I wanted to buy an old, distressed building as we did in Chicago and Nashville. Cheap loans keep our costs low and there's the added benefit of having our properties rise in value. When I couldn't find any buildings for sale with the right vibe, the developers of Ponce City Market, an amazingly cool organization called Jamestown Properties, kept coming back to us offering lower rent and more incentives. Finally, they offered such a great deal I could no longer refuse. The value of our brand was so high and differentiated that the landlord was willing to jump through hoops to include us in the overall development mix for its tenants. Playing hard-to-get worked wonderfully, albeit accidentally. We opened in Atlanta in June of 2016—a bit late when permit delays forced us to produce our first few shows at different sites—and now have all the foot traffic we could possibly want. The location is the best in Atlanta, the building's aesthetics are exactly what we always look for, and the mix of other stores and restaurants is a perfect fit for our brand.

Our Boston opening in 2017 was a nightmare of construction delays. We found a great spot on Canal Street, near the TD Garden, home of the Celtics and Bruins, on the ground floor of a new, twelve-story luxury apartment building. (A parking garage above us created perfect soundproofing.) My biggest mistake was using our Chicago contractor to do the job, because the close-knit local construction industry resented us greatly for that. Everyone from plumbers to delivery guys dragged their feet and gave us endless runarounds. Deadlines were missed, calls were not returned, and work days ended at 2 p.m. A project that should have taken five to six months limped along for twice that long. Our September 17 opening was pushed back to October, then to mid-November. We finally opened on November 21. The delays cost us more than $1 million for construction, refunding and rebooking tickets, and compensating artists. More than 5,000 ticket holders had to change their plans, but we bent over backwards to make it up to them. If someone had flown in from Toronto to see David Crosby, we flew them to our Chicago venue to see the show there instead (just the way Danny Meyer said we should in his book)!

Opening dates are particularly tricky in our business. When restaurants delay their grand opening, which happens all the time, nobody notices. But when you have the hard deadline of a scheduled show, there's nowhere to hide when faced with the usual contractor delays, cumbersome city bureaucracy, and other circumstances beyond your control. For a small company like ours, opening a 30,000-square-foot space for public assembly by a specific date is a huge challenge. Fortunately, Boston eventually forgave us, business is doing well, and I am trying to carve this lesson into my skin: Don't book an opening-night show until you are 100 percent sure the club will be ready! (And always hire local contractors!)

We opened in our sixth city, Washington, D.C., in June of 2018 without much delay. (Thought it took us another year to get an elevator permit!) Located in Ivy City, an industrial and residential neighborhood in the Northeast section, it's our biggest venue yet at 42,000 square feet, spread out over four floors. We expect it will be popular for private events as well as concerts and dinner. Ivy City is definitely a neighborhood in transition, but the influx of craft breweries, distilleries, and famous brands like Nike, Planet Fitness, and Target bodes well for its resurgence.

In each of our seven cities—we are entering Philadelphia in the fall of 2019—we are trying to reach deeper into the communities by launching smaller but highly profitable satellite locations that seat about 100 to 150 people. We did this with great success on two lovely waterfront promenades—Riverwalk on the Chicago River and Pier 26 on New York's Hudson River. (Another in Boston, on the Greenway near South Station, opened in the summer of 2019.) This strategy allows us to leverage the nearby "mothership" for wine-making and management and culinary expertise. Big crowds show up to sip wine and listen to music by the water as soon as the weather warms up, making these outposts a huge win for us.

Expanding around the country like this naturally required more capital, and today we have amassed seventy-five investors who have put up a total of about $20 million. Having lots of small investors—rather than a few big ones, as I did at the Knitting Factory—was definitely by design. It allowed me to live up to the promise I made to myself when I started City Winery: Remain in control to make sure my vision is well-executed and not hijacked by overzealous investors.

Now that City Winery is on such solid footing, however, that may change. As this book goes to press, I am considering giving up some control in our next round of financing in exchange for growth capital and a good employment contract in the interest of helping the company reach its full potential.

I should be clear that insisting on being in control did not mean that I thought I knew everything. As I assembled my board of directors, I made sure it was packed with trusted advisers—experts in real estate, finance, strategy, entrepreneurship, and the music industry, all accomplished people who could help City Winery grow and prosper over the long haul. What I did not want was shallow opportunists trying to make a quick buck, like those Vulture Capitalists of my dot-com days. Today, I treasure our quarterly board meetings as an important moment to absorb advice and perspectives that I could never obtain on my own. That's something I never had at the Knit, so thank you, Steve, Ilan,

Jim, Ken, Robert, Josh, Craig, and Ethan. I appreciate your time and commitment to the Company. (And, don't worry guys, I'll get back to work as soon as I finish the epilogue. ☺)

After nearly a decade of trying our best to "scale intimacy" at City Winery, it appears that we're doing a pretty good job. When Joan Osborne gave me that memorable New Year's Eve hug and thanked me for creating our first venue, I desperately hoped she would eventually say the same thing about *all* the clubs I hoped to open someday. I checked back with her recently to ask how we're doing, knowing she is the type of person who would definitely let me know if things were not up to snuff.

"We've played all the City Winery locations by now and they all have such a warm family atmosphere," she said. "Not just for the patrons, but also for the people who work there. I can tell you don't have high turnover because we see the same people over and over again. There's just a comfort level like, 'Okay, this is kind of like my living room, we are with family and friends and we can just relax and play music and have a great night.'"

Joan loves the fact that our clubs offer music fans a chance to escape their devices and hear from their favorite artists directly. "One thing I don't see at City Winery, that I see at every other place, is people filming the show on their phones," she told me. "The whole experience is about sitting down with your friends, your partner, or whoever. You're eating and drinking and you're really into the music, so you don't want to be on your phone. That is a cool thing."

When I hear comments like that, I often wonder what our secret sauce is, what we're doing right to create that delicate feeling of intimacy. I keep coming back to the importance of Basecamp. At our 2013 offsite in Puerto Rico, we required all managers to read Danny Meyer's book *Setting the Table* and talked a lot about his concept of enlightened hospitality, discussed at the beginning of this chapter. At that meeting, we came up with a set of "nonnegotiable values," including this definition of hospitality: "Empathic, intuitive, anticipatory, and proactive from every touch point in the company, from our marketing, sales, ticketing, onsite operation, concerts, private events, billing, and imagery. And obviously, our service staff." Danny has been such an inspiration that we still give copies of *Setting the Table* to all employees as part of their onboarding process. To date, we have handed out more than 2,000 copies!

It was at Basecamp in 2014 in Mexico (perhaps a good time to thank our airline sponsor, American Airlines) that I led seventy-five of our team members through an exercise to come up with our company mantra. After talking about everything we try to offer our guests, I asked the group for ideas of how to sum up our mission in a single pithy phrase—no more than two or three words—hoping to come up with our own version of "Just Do It" or "Think Different." From around the room came a flood of suggestions. On a whiteboard, I wrote them down—words like "passion" and "experience," which we discussed and debated. Many were close, but none seemed quite right.

Then Raul Mesias, our director of wine sales, shouted out, "Indulge Your Senses!"

It was an astonishing moment. I unbuttoned my shirt to reveal a T-shirt with those very words emblazoned on the chest. It was like one of those eerie stage magic tricks. People gasped, then started laughing. Raul and I were as shocked as anyone because we had not worked this out in advance. I had planned to reveal the T-shirt only after considering all the other options our staff offered. It was a dramatic example of what is possible when minds coalesce in a creative, organic, and symbiotic way, when you seem to actually absorb each other's thoughts.

I should probably clarify that this mantra, Indulge Your Senses, is not about living a life of selfish hedonism. Sure, we indulge, but we think it's important to give back too. That's a critical part of our culture. At Basecamp in January of 2018, we went back to Puerto Rico, but this time, our team-building exercise was to help that ravaged island recover from Hurricane Maria. During an advance trip there, farmers told me that beyond the ruined crops, structural damage, and loss of electricity, they had also lost a sense of joy. That really pained me, so in addition to attending to their material needs—raising $160,000 in donations; soliciting supplies like coffee, shovels, and extension cords; and sending our 125 managers to four farms to repair buildings and plant crops—we decided to do what we do best: put on a show.

First, we built a stage from fallen trees on a muddy patch of destroyed farmland out in the rainforest. Our supplier Meyer Sound donated a sound system; chef Juan Jose Cuevas of San Juan's Restaurant 1919, along with local chefs from the farm area, helped us create a feast; American Airlines provided airplane tickets; and Puerto Rican musicians from New York flew in to join local artists to make the phenomenal music. They were all incredible musicians, many alumni of bands led by the likes of Tito Puente, Ray Barretto, and Eddie Palmieri.

For one magical, unforgettable night—we called it a "Fiesta in the Fields"—the community and local farmers with their families came out for music, dancing, and locally sourced food. By the end, all fifteen cases of wine we brought were gone. Farmers thanked us with tears in their eyes, and we left feeling that, for one night at least, the people of that neglected island knew that their fellow American citizens cared.

That night now resides in our company's institutional memory, heightening that sense of intimacy we constantly strive for. And those good feelings contribute to the bottom line, the lifeblood of any business, allowing us to continue our important work. By 2019, a decade after the financial crisis wiped out my original business plan, the company was firing on all cylinders, with 1,400 employees helping to generate revenues approaching $100 million and operating profits (EBITDA) in double digits—which our board, year after year, wisely decides to plow back into the company to fuel further growth.

That growth includes a winery and private-event space in upstate New York, in the small village of Montgomery, which we plan to open in the fall of 2019; our new venue in Philadelphia, also scheduled for the fall; small outposts I am planning to call City Winery Tasting Rooms that can fit snugly in almost any urban environment; and a long list of cities in North America where we can locate our full 300-seat clubs, places like Toronto, Denver, Detroit, and Los Angeles—not to mention a hundred more cities around the world where our City Winery brand could thrive.

Just when everything seemed to be going smoothly, another disaster struck. In July of 2018, I was sitting at my desk in our New York office when I got a call from our land-lord, Trinity Church, informing me that it was leasing our entire block to a big media company I later learned was the Walt Disney Company, for $650 million. Disney would be tearing down all the buildings on the block to build its new headquarters.

This was not a complete shock. Every tenant in the red-hot real-estate market of Manhattan knows such dislo-cations can happen at any time. And Trinity Church, one of the largest landowners in the city, thanks to a huge gift of property from Queen Anne in 1705, had already tipped me off that something was in the works. But I was not prepared to have to move out by the summer of 2019. After lots of scrambling, I found the greatest location I could dream of, on Pier 57 at Hudson River Park, but these things take time. It wouldn't be ready until five or six months after we vacated. That means that, if you read this book around the time of its publication in the fall of 2019, we will be homeless in New York City, at best stuffed into a pop-up club and temporary offices until we can move into our new home.

In the end, we'll be fine. But when I got the word that we were being booted out of our flagship location, our birth-place, I was pretty upset. You see, Trinity had induced us to pour $2 million into an upgrade with promises that we could stay long enough to recoup the investment. Now our build-ing was about to be reduced to rubble. I wanted to yell at the

Church, "You can't screw me!" But I didn't. That's not how you talk to church people. Instead of serving them sacramental wine, as I once did, I served them a lawsuit in New York Supreme Court.

Finding Balance

When your company is based in the world of atoms, worrying about being dislodged from the space that generates most of your revenue can keep you up at night. Whether the threat comes from mendacious landlords, gyrations in the real-estate market, or natural disasters, you may sometimes fantasize about running a cloud-based firm with endless flexibility about where your customers and staff are located.

Don't. The most important variable in business is not whether your company is analog or digital but the quality of your relationships within that paradigm. That's true whether those relationships are with landlords or data centers, customers or users, employees or outsourcing firms. Being an ethical, considerate, trusted partner is always the best route to success in the long run, in my view, no matter what kind of business you're in. Not only does it feel better, but

I am convinced karma is real. "What goes around comes around," as they say. Some call that "Conscious Capitalism"; I just call it being a mensch.

And yet, in the short term, there's no doubt that, despite your best intentions, you can get screwed if you end up inadvertently doing business with scoundrels. That's pretty much what happened to us in the summer of 2018, when I realized that the ending of this book would have to be completely rewritten. That was the moment I learned that most of our New York operation—our corporate office and flagship venue in Tribeca—would have to relocate. The warm and trusting relationship we had with Trinity Church turned out to be anything but.

The good feelings between us had reached a high point in 2010, less than two years after City Winery opened in New York. I was having a fascinating conversation with the church rector, the Rev. Dr. James H. Cooper, about the religious traditions of wine-making. Wine has been used in Judeo-Christian rituals for millennia, of course, from Jesus turning water into wine to today's bris ceremonies, when a rag soaked in red wine is stuffed into a baby's mouth for him to suck on during the circumcision.

Rev. Cooper and I found it remarkable that kosher wine is often used to celebrate the Eucharist, a striking example of the common heritage shared by Christians and Jews. With both City Winery and Trinity Church so close to the site of the 9/11 attacks, we were both especially sensitive to the consequences of religious hatred and intolerance. So Rev. Cooper and I came up with an idea.

Why not have City Winery create a special sacramental Communion wine for the church? After all, Queen Anne had donated 250 acres of Manhattan farmland to Trinity in the early 1700s specifically for agricultural purposes. It was only through providence—or, you might say, dumb luck—that the area became a gold mine that transformed Trinity into a real-estate colossus worth a staggering $6 billion today. Why not honor the queen's generous bequest by producing a kosher vintage on this same land, to send a powerful message of affection and cooperation between two of the world's great religions?

"Brilliant," we said. "Let's do it." City Winery has always devoted about 20 percent of its production to wine made according to Orthodox Jewish law, so we selected a fermenting kosher barrel of Long Island Sauvignon Blanc, scheduled a ceremony, and invited the local media. On the appointed day, I ceremoniously removed the kosher seal from the barrel and Rev. Cooper and other members of the church added grape spirits, fortifying the wine for the next stage of its aging. Then they offered a humble blessing of thanksgiving. "Vicar's Vintage" was ready for bottling and ceremonial use by Christmas the following year.

Naturally, it was a huge disappointment, more than a decade later, to end up in a court fight with our beloved partner.

Things started to go south in July of 2018, when it was announced that Trinity was leasing our block to Disney for the next ninety-nine years in a deal valued at $650 million. At first, our conversations with our landlord were friendly enough. Rev. Cooper had retired by that time, but my contact at Trinity Real Estate was reasonable. Though Disney would be demolishing the whole block to make room for its new million-square-foot complex, the church would help us find a new space, he said, and let us stay for at least eighteen months, until January 2020, and possibly longer.

That was reassuring and perfectly consistent with our harmonious relationship. From the moment I signed our first lease in 2008, Trinity's leaders had always gone out of their way to be friendly and accommodating. I often golfed with members of their real-estate team at their private country club and chatted amiably when they came in to City Winery for lunch or a glass of wine. My lease did have a clause saying that, if the building is ever slated for demolition, we would have to vacate within twelve months, but Trinity repeatedly assured me that this was just a standard boilerplate clause that would most likely never get activated—and, even if it was, demolition projects take a long time and we would certainly get far more than twelve months' notice.

Over the past few years, however, things had become more complicated. In late 2016, Trinity told us that the top floor of our building was available—10,000 square feet just above City Winery in the two-story building—and made us an offer: Why not construct a rooftop bar, which would be a perfect fit for the upscale "Hudson Square" image they were promoting in the neighborhood? We could also renovate the second floor to create company offices and a 150-seat music venue called The Loft. We would have to pay the construction costs, but Trinity would give us rent abatements as compensation to encourage us to move ahead. The whole plan would cost us $2 million, but between the rent abatement and increased wine sales, we would earn that back in about three years; all profits thereafter would be gravy.

That pesky twelve-month demolition clause was still in the lease, but my friends at Trinity assured me it was safe to go ahead and invest the $2 million. Any new development on the block would not happen for at least three to five years, they said, possibly longer. That was consistent with our understanding over the previous decade, which was basically: Don't worry, we'll give you plenty of notice. I agreed to the terms, and in September 2017, we signed a five-year lease extension that included the second floor and roof.

At this point in the story, I should probably say that, after more than three decades in business, I'm a big boy. I know there are no guarantees in life and some people will sell out their own mother. Still, an often-overlooked truth about business is that much of it is based on trust. It's impossible to account for every eventuality in a contract—and the insanely high cost of lawyers means that, even if you set everything up perfectly in writing, you can still get screwed if you don't have as much money as your opponents to fight them in court. (That's what happened to me with Harvey Weinstein at one point—such a lovely fellow—but that's a story for another book.) The bottom line is that there comes a time in most business dealings when you just have to look your new partners in the eye and decide whether you trust them enough to take the plunge. In this case, it was not a tough call. After being in business together for so long, I completely trusted the pious folks of Trinity Church. Why should I doubt my golfing buddies and holy men with whom I shared sacramental wine?

We started construction and The Loft opened in June of 2018. A few months earlier, I decided to stop building the rooftop bar because Trinity informed us that a big media company had expressed interest in the property. By then, we were well underway, having already installed two staircases and an elevator shaft and had purchased a brand-new elevator. Trinity assured me that the deal was probably years away, but just in case, I told the construction crews to stop the job, at least temporarily.

When news about the Disney deal broke in July, I realized that I had just invested more than $2 million in a building that would soon be reduced to dust. Since Trinity had urged us to begin the work, given us many financial inducements to do so, and assured us that we could stay in the space for at least three years to earn back our investment, I was sure it would find a way to make us whole. I mean, $2 million is a lot of money to us, but not so much to a $6 billion church raking in $650 million on this deal alone. At the very least, I expected Trinity to live up to its word to give me at least eighteen months to move into a new home.

No such luck. Trinity curtly informed me that it was not our landlord anymore—all questions had to be directed to Disney. Our new landlord was polite enough but understandably eager to start knocking down buildings. We had little choice but to agree to vacate by July 31, 2019.

Meanwhile, I was scrambling madly to find a new space. I visited at least fifty sites, from midtown to Battery Park. As you might imagine, it's not easy to find spots that met our criteria: a 30,000-square-foot space without those clunky columns often found in Manhattan spaces that ruin sight lines; an accessible neighborhood; a landlord willing to dole out the necessary tenant improvement funds for the expensive renovation work. Soon, it was clear that there was no way I could have a new club up and running by the summer of 2019—especially our flagship New York venue that had to be created to perfection, the crown jewel of the City Winery chain.

My old friends at Trinity stopped coming by for lunch and wine and became harder and harder to reach. I checked my trail of communications to make sure I had not imagined the promises they made me. It was all there in writing. I had little choice but to take Trinity to court to recoup our $2 million investment—the first time I've ever sued anyone in my three decades of doing business. As this book goes to press, the church is fighting back vigorously, and I feel a bit like David going after Goliath. But it seems important to not back down. We're big enough now that we'll be fine, but a loss of $2 million could easily bankrupt a smaller company. I want this $6 billion church named after the Father, Son, and the Holy Spirit to think twice before stepping on any more little guys, as Manhattan's relentless pace of development marches on.

As I write this, I am anticipating a challenging latter half of 2019—finding a pop-up space to keep the music, wine, and cash flowing; moving into temporary offices; and searching for ways to pay my staff as our revenue drops. If you've read this far, you know I've been through much worse. In fact, I have no doubt that I will eventually look back on this period with deep gratitude because it pushed me and City Winery into a much better place.

Our Tribeca location, much as we loved it, was hardly the crown jewel of the chain. It had its charms—and a special place in my heart—but, as my first attempt at executing this nutty winery/music club/restaurant idea, it was definitely a practice run with many annoying imperfections. (Steve Earle complained that the heat was so high he got headaches, so he would hole up in his tour bus before shows to avoid our steamy dressing room.) Once the shock of our dislocation wore off, I was more than okay about the move. I became super excited.

That's because the space we picked is stellar—Pier 57 at Hudson River Park, a former maritime port at 15th Street and the West Side Highway. Our new landlord, RXR Realty, is transforming the historic structure into a sparkling mixed-use development at a cost of more than $400 million. We are the main retail/commercial tenant, sharing the building with one of the biggest technology companies in the world, Google. There is tremendous excitement in the city about the project and its special features like the grassy park on the roof overlooking the river, so I am expecting a lot of attention by the time we open in early 2020. Being under the spotlight will generate fantastic exposure and also put considerable pressure on me to make this the most awesome City Winery yet—like the second album from a new pop star who will suddenly get seriously scrutinized.

Fortunately, I've spent the last eight years learning how to build City Wineries from scratch, having completed eight of them now (plus four satellite venues), each one bigger and better than the last. Now I can put all that experience to good use. Pier 57 has a perfect location, a short Uber or Citi Bike ride from our previous spot downtown and accessible from many other parts of the city. (It also has parking for out-of-towners driving in on the West Side Highway.) The location is surrounded by many architecturally significant landmarks, including the Whitney Museum, Frank Gehry's striking IAC Building, structures by Danish architect Bjarke Ingels, and the surreal new Barry Diller Island park at Pier 55.

Our new space is phenomenal, a historic building with terrific views of the Hudson River and no columns blocking views of the stage. We have 32,000 square feet—enough to include a main dining/concert space seating about 350 that's roomier than our old place; a smaller, 150-seat venue still called The Loft; and a separate dining-only area seating up to 100 people with additional private dining spaces and a wine-tasting bar in a balcony with a dazzling view of the winery below. For the artists, we have two large dressing rooms, each with bathrooms, and a private dining room in the backstage area. At $10 million, the move will not be cheap, but we will not need to raise more investment capital. The costs will be covered by loans, tenant improvement allowances from the landlord, and cash flow.

One thing that gave me pause was the rent, which is three times what I was paying on Varick Street—and a far cry from my first Knitting Factory lease (which seemed high in those days at $1,800 a month!). But I'm confident that the higher rent will be more than offset by bigger and better private parties, larger lunch and dinner business, and more high-end VIP seating options, especially when big-name artists are playing. (We should also get a fair amount of business from the thousands of Google employees sharing our building.) As big brands know, there is tremendous marketing value in having a splashy flagship location in the buzzing media capital of New York.

Also giving me pause was the twenty-five-year lease that will not expire until I'm eighty-two, making this a legacy play that could last longer than I do. I know this sounds audacious—and it may just be the concert promoter in me talking—but I really think City Winery at Pier 57 can be the best music venue ever constructed in New York City, my own Carnegie Hall with a great wine list (with more than 1,200 bottles, it will be by far the largest in a US music venue). We all know how you get to Carnegie Hall. Well, I've been practicing for more than three decades now, so this could be my best chance to finally get there.

By 2020, when Pier 57 is up and running, we will be ready for further expansion—not just the dozens or hundreds of full-sized clubs in big cities in the US and abroad, from Los Angeles to Tokyo, but we are looking into building smaller venues for smaller urban areas like Pittsburgh and Raleigh, North Carolina. And we'll add more satellite venues, like Chicago Riverwalk and City Vineyard at Manhattan's Pier 26, near existing clubs. We may even achieve my vision of a chain of City Winery Tasting Rooms, where you can order flights of wine in a cozy 7,000- to 8,000-square-foot space with a music room, restaurant, and small wine-making facility.

I am constantly being asked by artists when will we open in places like Detroit or Denver or Milwaukee because that's what they are hearing from their fans. That's really cool—and an inspiration to move as quickly as possible before somebody else tries to reach those markets. Of course, you need to be a bit of a nut to add a full wine-making facility to the equation, but there's no doubt that the sight of a working winery, the smell of fermenting fruit, and the taste of wine drawn from French barrels gives us a special authenticity. Adding a winery makes our business plan very hard to copy, giving us a huge head start in satisfying the market we discovered.

In fact, the connection between music and wine goes far deeper than I ever imagined. It first struck me soon after we opened in New York, when *Food & Wine* magazine published a big photo spread of two great artists, the singer-songwriter Suzanne Vega and the superstar Spanish winemaker Alvaro Palacios. I watched in fascination as they sat on the City Winery stage and talked about their shared love of wine, food, music and art in such moving, poetic ways. Since then, I have seen it time and again—lovers of music are often lovers of wine, and both are passionate lovers of life. Suzanne has been a regular since our earliest days, and she is precisely the type of artist I wanted to fall in love with our clubs. Suzanne is more than a pop musician; she's also a sophisticated cosmopolitan who loves to cook, read, and enjoy wine—the quintessential City Winery demographic.

No conversation about wine and music would be complete without mentioning my friend Lou Reed, whose deep appreciation for both made him such an inspiration to me. I wanted to take a moment to remember Lou because he passed away in 2013, shortly after coming to my seder at City Winery. He was frail and needed help getting up on the stage. As he incanted the lyrics to Exodus by Bob Marley, he struggled—"Exodus, movement of Jah people"—but, after a few lines, his usual fire returned. He went off script a bit, but his reading was typical Lou, funny, powerful, and moving. I helped him off the stage and we hugged. That was the last time I saw him.

I have met so many other musical artists who love wine, people like Al Stewart, John Medeski, and Derek Trucks. They inspired me to start music-and-wine-pairing events at our clubs featuring a band performing the music of a particular artist while the audience samples the wine we selected to match it. We staged a "Zappa and Zinfandel" night and enlisted the great restaurateur and winemaker Joseph Bastianich to pair vintages with Led Zeppelin songs. For the Zeppelin event, "The Song Remains the Same" was paired with Champagne to match the song's bubbly introduction. Gimmicky? Maybe, but our audiences love it, and so does Bastianich. "I really believe in it," he said in an interview. "Wine and music are both unique because they both affect us in a visceral and emotional way."

For whatever mysterious aesthetic reasons, combining wine-making with live music is a winning formula. As we continue to grow, we are on pace to achieve $110 million to $120 million in revenue in 2020 and my Excel spreadsheets show us reaching $400 million to $500 million by 2026. Our EBITDA operating profit margins are very healthy at 10 percent of revenues, which should amount to more than $10 million in 2020. That's a fabulous fivefold return for our original investors—all still on paper at this point, because we continue to reinvest all profits back into the business.

To help us expand more quickly toward our full potential, we are now considering bringing in a big investor or group of backers willing to put up $25 million to $30 million. And, down the road, who knows? There could be an IPO or the sale of a controlling interest to a strategic partner. My main goal in creating City Winery, however, was never to sell it. I really wanted to make it "Built to Last," as the title of one of my favorite books, by management guru Jim Collins, puts it. One of the best ways to build a lasting business today is to find a healthy balance between the analog and digital worlds. That's why I wrote this book.

As a young entrepreneur, I got so caught up in the technology that I forgot that it's really just a tool to help you better serve the customer. Now that the term "Digital Revolution" feels passé, we are at a new social inflection point: The challenge is no longer choosing between the real and the virtual but weaving them together to achieve your goals.

"Customers don't wake up and think, I will be online this morning or offline later; we are rarely purely one or the other anymore and tend to jump constantly between two worlds without noticing," said José Neves, founder of the online luxury boutique marketplace Farfetch, in an interview with *The New York Times*. "Harnessing this behavior is a major challenge for retailers and brands."

Navigating this strange new world requires some deep thinking about what your business is really about. When people ask me, "What is your core business?" you might think it would be easy to answer. It's actually quite complicated. Some days, I think we're an urban winery that also puts on a great show and adds delicious food. Other days, I consider us the hippest entertainment company in the land, one that discovered a market of food-and-wine lovers that concert giants like Live Nation and AEG missed. The truth is that we're all those things, but I have come to realize that we are something else, too: a new form of media company.

I know, it sounded ridiculous to me, too, when it first occurred to me as I drifted into one of those dreamy states I sometimes slip into—with or without a glass of Pinot Noir. What could we possibly have in common with Disney, Viacom, Google, and Facebook, or smaller brands like Wine Spectator, or even mega-artists like Chance the Rapper or Taylor Swift who have practically become media entities unto themselves? Yet, the more I thought about it, the more logical it seemed.

What does a media company do? At its most basic, it brings content to audiences. That's exactly what City Winery does—only in person, while people eat and drink, using a stage occupied by the real Billy Bragg or Michelle Shocked rather than their disembodied digital representations. That must be why I've been casually referring to our stages as a "medium" since my earliest days at the Knitting Factory. And City Winery faces the same challenge every media company does: How to strike a harmonious balance between the worlds of atoms and bits. How can we cut through the media noise to bring in more customers? How can we use both the physical and virtual worlds to connect with fans before, during, and after the show? Can we add more digital elements to our live offerings—from video and audio streaming to recording shows—without alienating the artists and our fan base? These are the kind of questions all entrepreneurs, executives, and professionals must ask themselves at this confusing time, when no product or service is ever completely digital or completely analog.

Like any media company, we need more than customers to thrive—we need "fans." Fans, of course, love to gather at live events, whether at a theme park, Disney on Ice, book reading, or music concert. Have you noticed that rock bands never call their followers "customers"—or, even worse, "users," as Google or Facebook does? (Well, rock bands might have had "users," especially back in the sixties, but that's a different story.) The difference between a fan and a customer is clear: Fans will rave to everyone about how much they love the product—talking to a single friend or broadcasting to thousands through social media—while a customer is just someone who happens to buy something from you.

Our legions of devoted fans—500,000 nationwide and growing fast—are the key to our success. And the way we reach them offers a great example of how digital tools can be integrated into an analog product. Remarkably, after about one year of being open in a new market, we spend zero dollars on advertising, traditional or otherwise. Instead, we are in close touch with our fans—and followers of our performing artists—through our half-million email subscribers, social-media following, and millions of website visitors.

By proving a great place for artists to play and offering them a lucrative deal, we can offer our fans a tremendous variety of music, from big names to established niche artists to rising newcomers. (Though we are a media company, I will resist the urge to refer to their shows as "content"!) Thanks to Shlomo Lipetz, our vice president of programming (one of my first hires in 2008), the lineup of artists who have appeared at our clubs over the years is phenomenal: James Taylor, Art Garfunkel, Steve Martin on banjo with Edie Brickell, Aaron Neville, Norah Jones, Macy Gray, Shawn Colvin, Citizen Cope, Vernon Reid, Graham Nash, Neil Young, Allen Toussaint, Leo Kottke, Kurt Elling, Bettye LaVette, and many, many others.

Over the last two decades, the implosion of the record business has made it harder for artists to earn a living. But, as technology has made recorded music cheap and ubiquitous, it has also goosed the demand for live performances. Since Napster's debut in 1999, sales of concert tickets have skyrocketed from $1.5 billion to $8 billion in 2017. Music fans, increasingly unwilling to settle for digital reproductions, are demonstrating a powerful hunger for the real thing. And we're happy to give it to them.

We're also proud to offer these artists not just single gigs, but extended tours of all our clubs. This is especially helpful for older musicians whose fans want to see them in a warm, comfortable space. Joan Armatrading is a great example. Active on the scene since the early '70s, she understandably won't make the trip to the United States from her native England unless she can line up enough shows to make it worth her while. Enter City Winery, which can offer her a tour consisting entirely of dates at our venues. She can play four nights in each of seven cities and is quite happy to fly back home with more than half a million dollars. And thousands of her devoted fans are also happy for the chance to see her up close, in a small room.

In an exciting new media environment that requires physical presence and a human touch, City Winery is thriving. I'm not saying we have everything figured out. In many ways, we're still making it up as we go along. It's just thrilling to be making a healthy profit doing what I love—and not by resorting to the kind of illusory numbers you still see at some tech companies, even after two disastrous stock-market bubbles in as many decades. Today, it's actually a relief to speak in real financial jargon again, like multiples of EBITDA. I'm kind of embarrassed that acronym comes out of my mouth so fluently now. Some of my managers even kid me by calling it EBIDORF. But, after all that I've been through, it's such a thrill to be living in the real world again.

It's crazy when I realize that I've been putting on live shows in New York and around the country for more than three decades now, and somehow managed to create two iconic music brands along the way, in the Knitting Factory and City Winery. Sometimes, when I'm sitting at one of our clubs enjoying a glass of wine, I can't believe our success. Or that I'm a senior guy in the live-music industry now. That's absolutely mind-boggling to me. I still feel like a punk. Like I just got here.

Index

N

About the Author

City Winery founder and chief executive Michael Dorf dropped out of law school at age twenty-three to found New York City's Knitting Factory, which *The New York Times* later called "one of the most influential downtown music clubs of the 1990s." He was recognized as an Internet music pioneer by webcasting the first live music stream from a club anywhere in the world. In 2008, Michael brought together his love for music and wine by opening City Winery, Manhattan's first fully-functional winery, restaurant, music venue, and private event space. It now has thriving locations in Chicago, Atlanta, Nashville, Boston, Washington, D.C., and Philadelphia. Since 2006, his Carnegie Hall tribute concert series has raised more than $1.5 million to benefit music education programs. National media outlets have praised him as an important music impresario and *New York Magazine* lauded him one of the "10 Most Influential New Yorkers." Michael lives in Manhattan with his wife, the film producer Sarah Connors, and their three children.